Pelican Shared Writing

Non-Fiction Teacher's Book 6

Irene Yates

Series Editor: Wendy Body
Consultant: Julie Garnett

Pearson Education Limited
Edinburgh Gate
Harlow
Essex
CM20 2JE
England and Associated Companies throughout the World

ISBN 0582 50354 X
First published 2001

Printed in Great Britain by Scotprint, Haddington
Designed by AMR, Bramley, Hants

The Publisher's policy is to use paper manufactured from sustainable forests.

Longman
Edinburgh Gate
Harlow, Essex

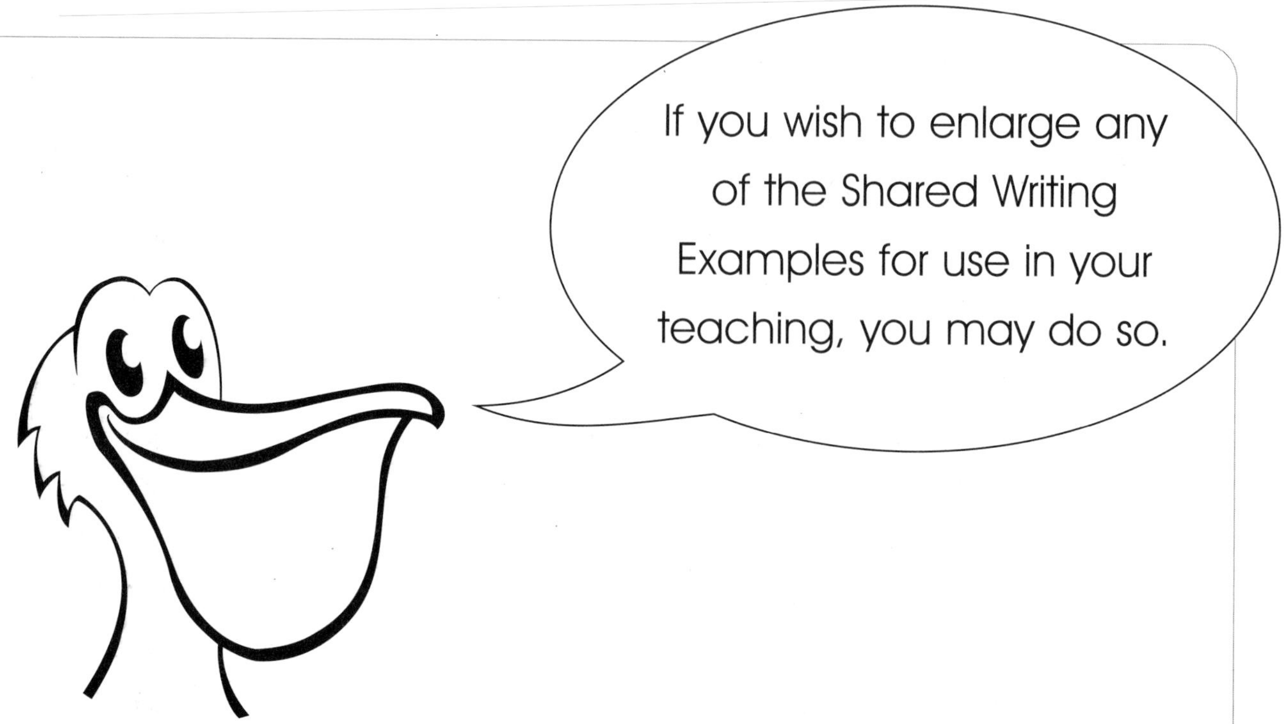
If you wish to enlarge any of the Shared Writing Examples for use in your teaching, you may do so.

Contents

Year 6 Non-Fiction Summary Chart	Page 4
What is Pelican Shared Writing?	Page 6
Teaching Shared Writing	Page 6
Teaching a Pelican Shared Writing Unit of Work	Page 7
ICT and Pelican Shared Writing	Page 8
Teaching Notes for Each Unit of Work	Page 10
1: Write an autobiography	Page 10
2: Write a biography	Page 12
3: Describe a person	Page 14
4: Write an obituary	Page 16
5: Develop a journalistic style	Page 18
6: Write a newspaper report	Page 20
7: Write a non-chronological report	Page 22
8: Revise and edit writing	Page 24
9: Compose an argument	Page 26
10: Present a formal argument	Page 28
11: Write a balanced report	Page 30
12: Summarise an argument	Page 32
13: Make notes 'for' and 'against'	Page 34
14: Make a contract	Page 36
15: Write a questionnaire	Page 40
16: Divide text into paragraphs	Page 44
17: Write notices	Page 46
18: Write an explanation	Page 48
19: Identify text types	Page 50
20: Select text type	Page 54
Copymasters C1–53	Page 56

Year 6 Non-Fiction Summary Chart

Text in Resource Book	Text level Objective	Sentence/Word level Objective	Unit of work
Term 1 Unit 1 Samuel Pepys – some facts about his life Samuel Pepys and the Great Plague of 1665 Writing a Biography	**T14**: to develop the skills of autobiographical writing in role	**W7**: to understand how words and expressions have changed over time	Write an autobiography
Term 1 Unit 2 Samuel Pepys – some facts about his life Samuel Pepys and the Great Plague of 1665 Writing a Biography	**T14**: to develop the skills of biographical ... writing in role	**S4**: to secure knowledge and understanding of more sophisticated punctuation marks; colons ... dashes	Write a biography
Term 1 Unit 3 Writing a biography Roald Dahl Roald Dahl – a letter	**T14**: to develop the skills of biographical ... writing in role		Describe a person
Term 1 Unit 4 Roald Dahl Roald Dahl – a letter	**T14**: to develop the skills of biographical ... writing in role ... e.g. a newspaper obituary	**S5**: to form complex sentence through, e.g.: using different connecting devices	Write an obituary
Term 1 Unit 5 The fox cub that was saved by a PC's helmet Journalistic writing	**T15**: to develop a journalistic style		Develop a journalistic style
Term 1 Unit 6 Samuel Pepys and the Great Plague of 1665	**T16**: to use the styles and conventions of journalism	**W7**: to understand how words and expressions have changed over time	Write a newspaper report
Term 1 Unit 7 Writing a Report Dry Earth – Deserts	**T17**: to write non-chronological reports linked to other subjects		Write a non-chronological report
Term 1 Unit 8 The fox cub that was saved by a PC's helmet	**T18**: to use IT to ... revise and edit writing write eg short extracts, and bring it to publication standard		Revise and edit writing
Term 2 Unit 9 Letter to the Editor Writing an Argument	**T18**: to construct effective arguments: developing a point logically and effectively	**S5**: to ... investigate conditionals ... use these forms to construct sentences which express, e.g. possibilities, hypotheses	Compose an argument
Term 2 Unit 10 Letter to the Editor Mobile Phones for Children	**T18**: to construct effective arguments: developing a point logically and effectively		Present a formal argument

Term 2 Unit 11 Meat Eating Versus Vegetarianism Writing a Balanced Report	**T19**: to write a balanced report of a controversial issue		Write a balanced report
Term 2 Unit 12 Meat Eating Versus Vegetarianism Writing a Balanced Report		**S4**: to revise ... contracting sentences	Summarise an argument
Term 2 Unit 13 Letter to the Editor		**S4**: to revise ... contracting sentences for note making	Make notes 'for' and 'against'
Term 2 Unit 14 Confusing Notices Making a Contract	**T20**: to discuss the way standard English varies in different contexts		Make a contract
Term 2 Unit 15 Television Watching Survey	**T20**: to discuss the way standard English varies in different contexts		Write a questionnaire
Term 3 Unit 16 Writing Paragraphs	**T21**: to divide whole texts into paragraphs, paying attention to the sequence and ... links		Divide text into paragraphs
Term 3 Unit 17 Public Notices		**S3**: to revise formal styles of writing: the impersonal voice	Write notices
Term 3 Unit 18 How wool yarn is made	**T20** to secure control of impersonal writing, particularly the sustained use of the present tense and the passive	**S3**: to revise formal styles of writing: the impersonal voice	Write an explanation
Term 3 Unit 19 Writing in different styles and forms Training your dog to 'sit' Little Greening Dog Show 'Do you want your dog to suffocate?' poster Dog Illnesses – Heat Stroke	**T22**: to select the appropriate style and form to suit a specific purpose and audience		Identify text types
Term 3 Unit 20 Training your dog to 'sit' Little Greening Dog Show 'Do you want your dog to suffocate?' poster Dog Illnesses – Heat Stroke	**T22**: to select the appropriate style and form to suit a specific purpose and audience		Select text type

Introduction

What Is Pelican Shared Writing?

Pelican Shared Writing is an easy-to-use resource for teaching shared writing. It comprises ten packs: one Fiction and one Non-Fiction pack for each year group for Years 2, 3, 4, 5 and 6. Each pack contains:

- one Writing Resource Book
- one Teacher's Book with copymasters
- a large sheet of acetate and a Pelican Page Clip

Each Writing Resource Book offers 20 units of work which cover all the NLS Writing Composition objectives for the year group. Each Writing Composition objective forms one unit of work. Links are also made to appropriate Sentence Level objectives.

Although *Pelican Shared Writing* stands alone, it has links to *Pelican Guided Reading and Writing* in terms of objectives and tasks and there are content links to *Pelican Big Books*.

The Writing Resource Books

- Each 48 page big book is split into three parts - one for each term's teaching objectives.
- Shared writing is rooted in shared reading, and so the Writing Resource Books contain the texts which not only provide the starting point for writing, but also act as models of the genre to be studied. Story plans and writing frames are sometimes included as well.
- There are quotes on and about the writing process from professional children's writers on the inside back cover of each Fiction Writing Resource Book. These are to initiate discussions on writing.
- The Non-Fiction Writing Resource Books have a summary of links to other areas of the curriculum on the inside back covers.
- Each book comes with a large sheet of acetate and a Pelican Page Clip for text marking and writing.

The Teacher's Books

The Teacher's Book in each pack contains:

- teaching pages for each Unit of work with detailed, step-by-step advice on what to do for each shared writing session. There are also examples of completed activities which teachers can use to guide the class in composing a text. Units will usually take more than one shared writing session to complete.
- a small number of copymasters e.g. writing frames, character planners. These are for general use and can also be applied to other texts and writing activities
- copymaster versions of all the Writing Resource Book texts. These can be used to make overhead transparencies and in instances where it is helpful for children to have their own copy of a text e.g. for annotation.

Teaching Shared Writing

Pelican Shared Writing complements the National Literacy Strategy's *Grammar for Writing* guidance. *Pelican Shared Writing* concentrates on delivering the text level Writing Composition objectives whereas *Grammar for Writing* concentrates on sentence level objectives. *Pelican Shared Writing* adopts a similar approach to shared writing which may be summarised as follows:

Key Features of Shared Writing:

- Make explicit how purpose and audience determine form and style.
- Link the writing to specific objectives.
- Rehearse sentences orally before writing.
- Discuss and explain alternatives and choices.
- Keep rereading to maintain flow, meaning and consistency.
- Involve children in the revision and editing.

Shared Writing Techniques:

Teacher Demonstration

The teacher composes and writes, modelling for children how to compose a particular text type or tackle a writing activity. He/she thinks aloud; rehearses choices before writing; explains choices and makes changes. The children do not contribute to the composition but they are invited to offer opinions on, for example, the choice of words or sentence construction. Demonstration time will vary according to the nature of the text and children's competence, but avoid spending too long – the children need to try things for themselves.

Teacher Scribing

The teacher acts as scribe and builds on the initial demonstration by getting the children to make contributions to the composition or task. The teacher guides, focuses, explains and challenges the contributions e.g. *Why did you choose that word? That's a really good sentence construction because ....* While children could make their contributions orally by putting up their hands, it is preferable for them to use whiteboards (in pairs or individually) which ensures participation by all children. It is also advisable to take "Time Out" i.e. get children to turn to each other in pairs and discuss possibilities for 30 seconds or so.

Supported Composition

Supported composition is preparation for independent writing. Children compose a limited amount of text using whiteboards or notebooks – in pairs or individually. Their alternatives are reviewed and discussed and choices and changes made. Some differentiation can be achieved by seating children in their ability groups and asking one group to compose one sentence orally, another to write one or two sentences and a third to write several sentences. Supported composition will enable you to identify those children who will need to repeat or continue the task in guided writing i.e. those who need greater support.

Shared writing is the most powerful means of improving and developing children's writing skills. But they will not develop into proficient writers unless two things happen. Firstly they are given sufficient TIME to practise the skills and craft of writing for themselves, and secondly, they receive the FEEDBACK which will help them evaluate what they have done and so learn from it.

Teaching a Pelican Shared Writing Unit of work

Support for each step will be found on the teaching pages

Discussing the Text for each unit

- Introduce the task and the objective
- Read the text in the Resource Book with the class and discuss the content
- Draw out features of the genre

↓

Shared Writing

- Demonstrate or model the particular features of the writing
- Scribe and guide the pupils' contributions
- Continue with supported composition by children working in pairs
- Check the children's learning

↓

Independent Writing

- Children complete the writing task.
- They consolidate their learning by carrying out another similar task.

↓

Checking the Objective

- Determine children's understanding of the objective and how far they can apply their knowledge by evaluating their writing.

↓

Revisiting the Objective

- If needs be, repeat the whole process using the suggested activity.

Note: A Pelican Shared Writing CD-ROM is available for use alongside each year's work. For further details, please see the section on ICT, overleaf.

ICT and Pelican Shared Writing

ICT may be used by all pupils to support writing skills. The word processor or desktop publishing package can enable the child to focus on the development of ideas and the manipulation of the written word without the physical constraints imposed by the handwriting process. The ease of editing, the spell-checking facilities and the ability to move text around the page make ICT support programs valuable tools to include within the writing repertoire. Writing tasks offer the ideal opportunity to integrate and apply those ICT skills being developed in the ICT curriculum.

Almost any writing task may be approached using ICT as an optional writing tool. These writing tasks will offer strong links with the ICT curriculum, which aims for pupils to:

- 'develop their ability to apply their IT capability ICT to support their use of language and communication'
- 'pass on ideas by communicating, presenting and exchanging information'
- 'develop language skills eg in systematic writing and in presenting their own ideas'
- 'be creative and persistent'
- 'explore their attitudes towards ITC, its value for themselves ... and their awareness of its advantages and limitations'

(QCA Scheme of Work for ICT, Aims and Purposes)
The 'Communicating' strand for ICT is inextricably linked with developing literacy. Computer access is a great resource for independent, group and class work, and is too valuable a tool to remain unused during the development of literacy skills. It is a great motivator and encourages collaborative work that can become more focused as children's attention is extended.

Within the suggested Year 6 Non Fiction Pelican Shared Writing activities, there are some clear links with Unit 4A 'Writing for Different Audiences', from the QCA Scheme of Work for ICT. This Unit focuses on text manipulation skills. The writing activities offer ideal opportunities for the application of these ICT skills. The presentation of work may also be developed in the multimedia setting, and link to Unit 6A 'Multimedia Presentations'. Other links may be found in:

Unit 5B (Analysing Data and Asking Questions)
Unit 6D (Using the Internet to search large databases and to interpret information)

Links to the most relevant National Curriculum Programme of Study for ICT are listed in the table opposite.

The differentiated writing frames for Year 6 (Fiction and Non-Fiction) are available on the CD-ROM entitled Pelican Shared Writing Year 6 (ISBN 0582 50955 6), which can be easily installed on any machine supporting Microsoft Word. Here they may be adapted, should you so wish, to suit your particular needs. The CD-ROM also provides cross-referencing charts for both Writing and ICT targets, including the ICT Programme of Study references and links to the QCA Scheme of Work for ICT – collated and readily available for inclusion into planning records.

Year 6 Non-Fiction
Relevant objectives from the ICT Programme of Study

Pupils should be taught:

1b
how to prepare information for development using ICT, including selecting suitable sources, finding information, classifying it and checking it for accuracy (*for example, finding information from books or newspapers, creating a class database, classifying by characteristics and purposes, checking the spelling of names is consistent*)

2a
how to develop and refine ideas by bringing together, organising and reorganising text, tables, images and sound as appropriate (*for example, desktop publishing, multimedia presentations*)

3a
how to share and exchange information in a variety of forms, including e-mail (*for example, displays, posters, animations, musical compositions*)

3b
how to share and exchange information in a variety of forms, including e-mail (*for example, displays, posters, animations, musical compositions*)

4b
describe and talk about the effectiveness of their work with ICT, comparing it with other methods and considering the effect it has on others (*for example, the impact made by a desktop-published newsletter or poster*)

National Curriculum for England, ICT Programme of Study

Term 1 Unit of work 1:

Write an autobiography

Resource Book pages 2–6

Writing Objective

T14: To develop the skills of ... autobiographical writing in role, adopting distinctive voices.

Links to Sentence/Word Level Work

W7: To understand how words and expressions have changed over time.

Text Copymasters: C7–11

Discussing the Text:

- Ensure that the children understand the difference between a biography and an autobiography.
- Tell the children who Samuel Pepys was if they do not know (an administrator for the British Navy, who lived in the 17th century and is well-known for the detailed diaries that he wrote about his life).
- Read through the texts on Resource Book pages 2 to 6. ‘Samuel Pepys – some facts about his life’ and ‘Samuel Pepys and the Great Plague of 1665’.
- Explain the task to the children, which is to write diary entries in role as Mrs. Pepys, thus providing some of *her* autobiography.
- *How will the entries be written?* In the first person. In the same kind of language as the texts provide, not in contemporary language.
- Read through the texts again. This time, discuss all the information that you can extract which is relevant to Mrs. Pepys.
- Discuss how Mrs. Pepys might have been thinking and feeling at the time of each diary entry.

Shared Writing

Teacher Demonstration

- Reminding the children that you are writing diary entries and writing in role using Mrs. Pepys’ voice, look for an interesting starting point for her diary. *What might her view have been of the incident described on 1st January 1660? How might she speak? How might her speaking be translated into writing?*
- Date, compose and write your first entry, explaining again that you are writing in the *first person*. (See Shared Writing Example opposite.)
- Compose and write a second entry, taking information from the text in chronological order.

Teacher Scribing

- Read through the next part of the text with the children. How would Mrs. Pepys have felt about meeting the Queen?
- Discuss points which would make interesting entries and give the children plenty of time and opportunity to verbalise the points into first person sentences. (See Shared Writing Exampl.) *How do we need to start?*
- Take suggestions from the children for further entries and scribe them.

Supported Composition

- Give the children Time Out in pairs to discuss and write one or two further entries.
- Check and compare.

Shared Writing Example: **The Journal of Mrs. Pepys**

1660

Jan I have tried so hard to be a good wife to my husband, Samuel, but today I fear I showed that I am lacking in certain skills. We were to have turkey for dinner and I am afraid that in preparing it I burned my hand and did not make a good job of it at all.

Jan Though my hand is hurting and bandaged, I have done my very best today, making the fire in the drawing room and washing my husband's clothes with my bare hands. How glad I shall be when we can afford to hire some help.

Nov How exciting it was to be in the presence of Her Majesty, the Queen! I was dressed in my finest gown though I fear she didn't even notice me for I was placed behind her chair - but to be close enough that, had I but put out my hand - I would have touched her!

April 23rd 1661 Oh, such a day! The coronation of our sovereign King, Charles II - and I was there, beside my husband! Such a spectacle! Oh, the finery! The jewels and gems! The ladies and gentlemen! Such a wonderful day I don't think it will ever be surpassed in the whole of my life!

Independent Writing

- Write entries in Mrs Pepys' diary for June 11th 1664 and August 1665.

Checking Children's Learning

- Can the children tell you the difference between *biography* and *auto-biography*?
- Can the children explain the difference between *first person* and *third person*?
- Have the children written their diary entries in an appropriate voice?

Revisiting the Objective

- Write entries in Samuel Pepys' diary for September 1666, the Great Fire of London.
- Using the Outline for a CV on Copymaster C1, write a Curriculum Vitae for Samuel Pepys.

Term 1 Unit of work 2:

Write a biography

Resource Book pages 2–7

Writing Objective

T14: To develop the skills of biographical ... writing in role, e.g. of historical characters, through composing a biographical account based on research.

Links to Sentence/Word Level Work

S6: To secure knowledge and understanding of more sophisticated punctuation marks: colon ... dashes.

Text Copymasters: C7–11

Discussing the Text:

- Check the children's knowledge about biography and autobiography.
- Recap on the work that was done in the last session, and discuss the information that they can remember about Samuel Pepys and his wife. *Who was Samuel Pepys? When did he live? Why is he famous?*
- Explain the task to the children, which is to write a brief biography of Samuel Pepys.
- Read through and discuss the prompt sheet on page 7 of the Resource Book, 'Writing a Biography'. Look at the use of colons and dashes on this sheet, and discuss how they might be used in the Shared Writing.

Shared Writing

Teacher Demonstration

- Keeping the prompt sheet on display, and referring to it when necessary, compose and write the opening of the biography. (See Shared Writing Example.) Ask the children what event should be referred to at the beginning. (Pepys' birth.)
- Return to the texts on pages 2 to 6 for information when you need to. If possible, have other sources on Samuel Pepys available for reference.
- Compose and write the next sentence.

Teacher Scribing

- Using the prompt sheet and the information texts with the children, discuss what you might write in the third sentence. *What historical event did Pepys witness in 1648?*
- Ask the children to verbalise the next two or three sentences and scribe them. *Don't forget, we can use phrases such as 'after so and so' or 'when he had done this'.*

Supported Composition

- In pairs, children add another important event to the biography.
- Check and compare. Choose texts to add.

Shared Writing Example:

Samuel Pepys

Samuel Pepys was born on February 23rd, 1633. He is famous for keeping a diary, in which he detailed so many historical facts and events that the diary is used as an important source for historians.

In 1648, Pepys was at the execution of Charles I. He married in 1655 and later became a clerk at the Exchequer – so he was quite an important person in London.

On January 1st 1660, Pepys began his diary. It was written in shorthand and contained details about the daily life of the period, and his own intimate feelings. He continued the diary until 1669, when he was forced to give up because of his poor eyesight. His diaries include descriptions and minute detail about the Plague and the Great Fire of London. Once the diaries were deciphered, in 1825, his eyewitness accounts gave historians access to information that they would otherwise never have found.

Pepys died in 1703.

Independent Writing

- Give the children time and opportunity to complete the biography.

Checking Children's Learning

- Can the children tell you two or three sources of information when writing a biography?
- Can the children tell you the purpose of a biography?
- Can the children explain some of the text features of a biography?

Revisiting the Objective

- Use some of the information contained in the texts and gathered from other research to begin a biography of Mrs. Pepys.

Term 1 Unit of work 3:

Describe a person

Resource Book pages 7–13

Writing Objective

T14: To develop the skills of biographical ... writing in role ... e.g through describing a person from different perspectives, e.g. school report.

Text Copymasters: C12–18

Discussing the Text:

- Recap on the work the children have done on writing biographies and check their knowledge. If necessary, run through with them again the prompt sheet 'Writing a Biography' (Resource Book page 7).
- Explain the task, which is to read through a biographical text and, using this information, to work out what the person's school report might have been like. The children will then be asked to write the school report.
- Read through the texts about Roald Dahl on Resource Book pages 8 to 13 (Text Copymasters C13 to 18). Encourage the children to gather more material about this writer from other sources, e.g. Dahl's autobiography 'Boy'. Distribute copies of Copymaster C2, or display as an OHT.
- *What ideas can we gather about Roald Dahl's progress at school, from the information in these texts? For example, it is easy to see from the letter to his mother that he was not very good at spelling when he was nine. What else might we infer from the texts?*
- Decide the format of your school report, or show the children Copymaster C3.

Shared Writing

Teacher Demonstration

- *It tells us in the text that Roald Dahl did not get on very well at school. What might we infer from this?* Compose and write the reports for Maths, Latin and French. (See Shared Writing Example opposite.)
- Focus on the structure and features of school report writing, e.g: Note form, abbreviations such as 'G' for Good and 'VG' for very good.

Teacher Scribing

- Take suggestions from the children for Geography, History and Science and scribe them. *What can we tell from the information we have? We may have to surmise, or imagine.*

Supported Composition

- Children write the entry for English (to include spelling), and for P.E.
- If using Copymaster C3, you may also suggest that the children insert 'grades' in the right-hand column. Explain to them how they should do this.
- Share, select and scribe.

Shared Writing Example:

Half-termly report from:	**Saint Peter's School**
Name: Year: Term:	Dahl, Roald 1928 Spring Term
English:	*Dahl has a natural way with language, His compositions are very imaginative but he needs to learn to spell properly. He should put in more effort.*
Maths:	*Room for improvement.*
Latin:	*More effort and concentration needed.*
French:	*There is a little improvement.*
Geography:	*Dahl seems to have an interest in the subject, but needs to apply himself more.*
History:	*Room for improvement.*
Science:	*Weak, does not work hard enough.*
Physical education:	*VG. A good all-rounder, enthusiastic and energetic.*
Conduct:	*Fairly good, with some lapses. If he put in a bit more effort he would get on a lot better, both intellectually and socially, as well as psychologically .*
Term ends on: March 10th	
Signed: *A.L.Wilkins*	

Independent Writing

- Children complete the report, using additional sources, e.g. 'Boy', for information.

Checking Children's Learning

- Can the children tell you how a school report is written?

Revisiting the Objective

- Go back to the biographical material on Samuel Pepys in Units 1 and 2 (Resource Book pages 2 to 6), and make up a school report for him.
- Can the children tell you the perspective of a school report?

Term 1 Unit of work 4:

Write an obituary

Resource Book pages 8–13

Writing Objective

T14: To develop the skills of biographical ... writing in role ... e.g. through describing a person from different perspectives, e.g. a newspaper obituary.

Links to Sentence/Word Level Work

S5: To form complex sentences through, e.g.: using different connecting devices.

Text Copymasters: C13–18

Discussing the Text:

- Explain to the children what an obituary is (an account of someone's life, written soon after their death).
- Recap on biographies so that children can see the connection.
- Explain the task, which is to write together an obituary for Roald Dahl, using the information in the texts (Resource Book pages 8 to 13) and any other information the children can gather.
- The main features of an obituary are that it is usually respectful and objective; it is formal; it gives the main events and achievements of a person's life (usually in chronological order); it often contains a tribute. It gives the time and place of birth and death and (if known) the cause of death.

Shared Writing

Session 1

Teacher Scribing

- *First we need to make notes of the events of Roald Dahl's life.* Go through Resource Book pages 8 to 12 with the children, extracting points of information and scribing them. (See Shared Writing Example 1, below.)
- You can also draw on the information on Copymaster C2.

Supported Composition

- Children write two or three points of their own. Can they bring any more information to the notes from their knowledge and reading? *Can you find a list of Roald Dahl's books?*
- What extra information can be gathered from the letter on page 13?
- Check and compare, then choose items for the notes.

Shared Writing Example:

1. Notes from pages 8 to 12:

Born, 1916, in Wales, parents Norwegian
2nd WW fighter pilot
So tall could hardly fit cockpit
Shot down enemy planes
Crashed, back-ache all his life
Posted to Washington, USA, 1942
Met American author CS Forester who asked for ideas for flying stories
Dahl wrote stories, CSF got them published
Plus: Sent to boarding school when he was 9 and wrote to mother every week

Married Patricia Neale, film actress, 1953
4 daughters + 1 son
Son, Theo had tragic accident, 1960
Olivia died of measles, aged 7, 1962
Dahl began to write chn's stories
Cared particularly about his readers
Answered all letters
Sadness and ill fortune
Made children laugh
Wrote many children's books
Died 1990, Oxford

Session 2
Teacher Demonstration

- Read the notes through carefully with the children.
- Reminding the children of the features of an obituary, compose and write an opening paragraph, summarising his achievement. Help the children to form complex sentences, joined with different connecting devices (e.g. although ... because ...).

Supported Composition

- Give the children Time Out, in pairs, to work out and verbalise a second paragraph.
- Children to write their paragraph.
- Check and compare.

Shared Writing Example:

Roald Dahl

Born: 1916, Cardiff
Died: 1990, Oxford

No one could have known, when he was at school, that Roald Dahl would become one of the most famous and best-loved children's writers of all time. Although he had sadness and ill-fortune in his life, Roald Dahl's stories have kept children all over the world reading – and laughing. Many of his famous children's books have been made into succesful films. These include *Charlie and the Chocolate Factory, Matilda and the Witches*.

Born in Wales, to Norwegian parents, and sent to boarding school at the age of 9, Roald Dahl didn't get on very well at school.

In the 2nd World War he became a fighter pilot, shooting down enemy planes, despite the fact that he was so tall he could hardly fit into the cockpit of the planes – until he crashed. The crash meant that he suffered backache for all of his life.

In 1942 he was posted to Washington, USA, where he met American author C.S. Forester, who asked him for ideas for flying stories. Dahl wrote some stories, and the author was so impressed that he arranged to have them published.

In 1953, Dahl married Patricia Neale, the film actress, and they had four daughters and a son. His son, Theo, had a tragic accident in 1960. Because of this accident, Dahl, together with a friend, invented a machine to take fluid away from injured brains. This machine, the Wade-Dahl-Till valve, saved hundreds of lives. One of his daughters, Olivia, died of measles, aged 7, in the 60s.

Independent Writing

- Children complete the obituary.

Checking Children's Learning

- Can the children tell you at least two different types of biographical writing?

Revisiting the objective

- Write an obituary for Samuel Pepys, using the information on Resource Book pages 2 to 6.

Term 1 Unit of work 5:

Develop a journalistic style

Resource Book pages 14–16

Writing Objective:
T15: To develop a journalistic style.

Text Copymaster:

Discussing the Text:

- Explain the task to the children, which is to write, in journalistic style, a piece for a local newspaper about a local animal issue.
- Check the children's knowledge. *What do we know about writing for newspapers?* (It has to be punchy and attract the reader's attention. It needs to provide correct information.)
- Read and discuss the article about the fox cub on Resource Book pages 14 and 15 (Text Copymasters C19 and C20).
- Read and discuss the prompt sheet 'Journalistic Writing' on Resource Book page 16 (Text Copymaster C21).
- Brainstorm ideas for the content of the article and arrive at an agreement. If you wish, you might suggest the topic in the Shared Writing Example – which is an article about a brood of ducklings who cross the road every morning and hold up the traffic.

Shared Writing

Teacher Scribing

- Using the Resource Book article as a model, and the prompt sheet as a guide, take suggestions from the children for a snappy heading to the article and scribe. Encourage the children to use alliteration or to think of a pun or a play on words (See Shared Writing Example).
- Make up a by-line and scribe it.
- Returning as necessary to the prompt sheet and text, take suggestions from the children for an opening paragraph. *How can you describe the event in a short, interesting paragraph?* (See Example).

Supported Composition

- In pairs, using the prompt sheet as a guide, children write the next paragraph, stating the facts.
- Check and compare.
- Choose ideas and sentences to add to the text.

NB: Keep your Shared Writing for further use in Unit of Work 8.

Shared Writing Example:

Ducks Drive Drivers Quackers

By Ivor Beake

Every morning at eight o'clock, just as rush-hour is getting into full flood, Daisy Duck, of Upton Farm, waves a wing at the drivers and leads her brood across Belvedere Way to reach the pond just in front of the pub, the Dipping Inn.

There are eleven ducklings this year and each of them follows Daisy in single file as she waddles unceremoniously along.

Cars line up as far as the crossroads, hooting their horns and flashing their lights, but Daisy ignores them all. 'As far as Daisy's concerned,' says Evie Feathers, the farmer, 'getting across to that pond is the only thing that matters. The drivers can hoot and flash their lights as much as they like but it won't stop her!'

Things are now so bad that the Council is erecting a sign to show that the ducks crossing have right of way.

Mr. Paul Thomas of Belvedere Close said, 'There's no other way round to the main road. I'm late for work every morning and my boss is getting fed up with the excuse. But what can I do?'

I asked Daisy could she perhaps think of making a later start – after the rush-hour. And her reply?

'Quack! Quack! Quack!' I take that as a No.

Independent Writing

- Children to finish the article, including quotes if possible.

Checking Children's Learning

- Can the children tell you some of the features of journalistic writing?
- Use the prompt sheet to check that all the features of journalistic writing are present in the children's articles.

Revisiting the Objective

- Take another of the ideas suggested during the brainstorming session and repeat the process.

Term 1 Unit of work 6:

Write a newspaper report

Resource Book pages 4–6 and 16

Writing Objective:

T16: To use the style and conventions of journalism to report on real …
or imagined events.

Links to Sentence/Word Level Work

W7: To understand how words and expressions have changed over time.

Text Copymasters: C9–11 and C21

Discussing the Text:

- Recap on the children's knowledge of journalistic writing *What is its purpose? How do we go about writing it?* Show them again the prompt sheet on Resource Book page 16, 'Journalistic Writing'.
- Explain the task, which is to write a journalistic text as in the last session, but this time using the text on Resource Book pages 4–6 ('Samuel Pepys and the Great Plague of 1665') as a source of information.
- Discuss the 'tone' to be used with the children. *Although it is journalistic writing, it wouldn't be right to use the same 'tone' as for our animal article, because the content is much more serious. Think about feelings and empathy.*
- Discuss the purpose – to give the readers information about the Great Plague.
- Reread together Resource Book pages 4–6.

Shared Writing

Teacher Scribing

- Brainstorm ideas for a short, arresting headline and scribe it (See Shared Writing Exmple opposite).
- Take suggestions for, and scribe, a byline.
- *How would someone begin to describe something so sad?* (With the facts, perhaps followed by a description of people's reactions to them.) Take suggestions from the children for an opening paragraph and scribe it.

Supported Composition

- Refer the children back to the prompt sheet 'Journalistic Writing' (Resource Book page 16).
- In pairs, children write a further paragraph giving figures and details of the events as they are happening. *Try to include a quote.*
- Check and compare.

Shared Writing Example:

PLAGUE TAKES GREATER TOLL!

By William Wandsworth

Yet more deaths.

In London today, there is only sadness and fear. So many people have died of the plague now that the church bells are hardly ever silent.

In the week ending 31st August, 1665, six thousand, one hundred and two people fell victim. This is a huge rise from the numbers at the beginning of July, during the first week of which only 500 people died. The plague has taken a great hold and no one can foresee its end.

Mr. Samuel Pepys, who is keeping a daily journal of events, told our reporter last night, 'People are so afraid and desperate that they are sending their children to live with friends, as far from the heart of the city as possible. They hope that this will save them. The children are handed over naked so that they do not carry the plague with them on their clothing.'

Estimates are that of London's 400,000 inhabitants, at least 100,000 will be lost before the plague can be contained.

Independent Writing

- Children write a closing paragraph for the article.

Checking Children's Learning

- Can the children explain 'journalistic style' to you?
- Can the children tell you the differences and similarities between this article and the animal article?

Revisiting the Objective

- Use a different piece of historical text to repeat the process.

Term 1 Unit of work 7:

Write a non-chronological report

Resource Book pages 17–21

Writing Objective:
T17: To write non-chronological reports linked to other subjects.

Text Copymasters: 22–26

Discussing the Text:

- Read together the text 'Dry Earth – Deserts (Resource Book pages 18–21).
- *How have the animals in the text adapted to suit their environment?* (e.g. Their bodies conserve as much water as possible. They have also adapted their behaviour.)
- Explain the task to the children, which is to write a report that is linked to this subject. Suggestions might be: *how the fox has adapted to urban living; how the hedgehog has adapted to traffic.* Ask the children for other suggestions and decide upon a subject.
- Recap on children's knowledge of non-chronological report writing. (It is organised without reference to a sequence of time. Instead it may be organised by characteristics and features, for example.)
- Read together the prompt sheet 'Writing a Report' on Resource Book page 17.
- Reread the 'Dry Earth' text, identifying relevant features as you go.
- Tell the children that you are now going to write a non-chronological report toegther. Ask them to help you to choose a topic. This could be a subject currently being studied in another area of the curriculum. Or you might like to choose another 'animals' topic, but one which is closer to home – e.g. the urgan fox. (See Shared Writing Example.)
- Decide which topic to write about, keeping a note of the others for future use.
- Gather information on the chosen subject from various sources.

Shared Writing

Teacher Scribing

- Keeping the prompt sheet in mind, and using the text on pages 18–21 as a model, take suggestions from the children for a general opening statement about the chosen subject and scribe it.
- Take suggestions for sub-headings and jot them down.
- Take suggestions for the second paragraph and scribe it.

Supported Composition

- In pairs, give the children Time Out to discuss what the next paragraph and subheading will be, and to verbalise and then write it. *Don't forget to use the prompt sheet 'Writing a Report', and the model 'Dry Earth – Deserts', to help you.*
- Repeat this process for further paragraphs.
- Check and compare.

NB: Keep your Shared Writing for use in Unit of work 8.

Shared Writing Example:

The Urban Fox

The natural habitat of the fox is the countryside. However, with towns and cities growing and sprawling further and further into rural areas, they have managed to adapt themselves to urban living.

What is a fox?

A fox is really a member of the small wild dog family. It lives in Africa, Asia, Europe, North America and South America. Foxes are scavengers. They live on all kinds of small animals, from worms to rabbits. They also eat berries.

Appearance

The common fox is red in colour with black patches behind the ears and a light tip on its tail. Its body is about 60 cm long. It also has a tail, which is called a 'brush, about 40 cm long. It has a long, narrow snout.

Habits

Foxes are mostly nocturnal animals, hunting at night. They live in underground 'dens', often using the abandoned burrows of other animals, in which they rear their young.

The Town Fox

The fox has adapted himself easily to town life. Unwary pet owners are horrified to find that he scavenges in gardens for chickens, ducks and rabbits. He tips the lids off dustbins and eats whatever he can find. He slinks through the towns and cities under cover of darkness, and is known to be very crafty and very cunning.

Independent Writing

- Children write a conclusion to their reports and illustrate them with pictures or diagrams.

Checking Children's Learning

- Can the children tell you the main features of report writing?
- Can the children prepare a report from gathered information?

Revisiting the Objective

- Using the prompt sheet and the text as a model, take the second of the children's suggestions for a subject and repeat the process.

Term 1 Unit of work 8:

Revise and edit writing

Resource Book pages 14–15

Writing Objective:
T18: To use IT to ... revise and edit writing ... and bring it to publication standard, e.g. through compiling a class newspaper.

Text Copymasters: C19–20

Discussing the Text:

- Explain the task to the children, which is to use IT to revise the texts written in in Units 5 and 7 as content for a class newspaper.
- *We could produce a class newspaper. We will call it 'Issues' and write about various things that are newsworthy.*
- Read through the texts produced in Units of Work 5 and 7. Look at, and discuss, the differences between them. *The Unit 5 piece was written for a newspaper so we can probably use it as it is (See Shared Writing Example 1). We need to decide on headlines, fonts, etc. then key the text in. The Unit 7 piece, a report, needs editing for our newspaper. We must make it clear, concise and to the point.*

Shared Writing

Teacher Scribing

- First, look at the title of the Unit 7 piece and take suggestions for turning it into a short and arresting headline. (See Shared Writing Example 2.)
- Take suggestions for size, properties and choice of font.
- Reminding the children that the report is being revised to fit a more journalistic approach, take suggestions for rewriting the opening paragraph, and key in. *Can we change the order of the paragraphs? Can we join any sentences? Can we make it more concise? Can we change the subheadings to make them more arresting? Do we need all the information? Can we add anything?*

Supported Composition

- Ask the children, in pairs, to revise and key in subsequent paragraphs.
- Print off each piece of revised work.
- Check, compare and choose a piece to add to the class newspaper.

Independent Writing

- Children write further newspaper articles, on the theme of 'animals'.

Checking Children's Learning

- Can the children tell you how they can make a piece of newspaper text look good, using IT?
- Can the children tell you how to turn a report into a newspaper article?

Revisiting the Objective

- Using IT, revisit the work the children did in Units 3 and 4. Edit and present the texts to provide another feature for the class newspaper.

Shared Writing Example 1:

ISSUES ... the magazine for people who care

Mr. Fox Comes To Town!

By Adam Quick

The natural habitat of the fox is really the countryside but, with towns and cities growing and sprawling further and further into rural areas, he has managed to adapt himself to urban living.

Meet Mr Fox

A fox is really a member of the small wild dog family. He is found in Africa, Asia, Europe, North America and South America. Foxes are carnivores and scavengers, living on all kinds of small animals, from worms to rabbits, as well as berries when nothing else is available.

He's red in colour with black patches behind the ears and a light tip on his tail. He is about 60 cm long plus a tail, which is called a 'brush', about 40 cm long, and has a long, narrow snout. Foxes are mostly nocturnal animals, hunting at night. They live in underground 'dens', often using the abandoned burrows of other animals in which to rear their young.

The Urban Fox

The urban fox has adapted himself easily to life in town. Don't leave your pets outside at night because he will soon find your chickens, ducks and rabbits. He will tip the lid off your dustbin and eat whatever he is lurking there.

You might just catch sight of the end of his brush as he slinks through the town under cover of darkness. But you won't have much luck catching the very crafty and very cunning Mr. Fox because he will easily outrun you.

Shared Writing Example 2:

Ducks Drive Drivers Quackers

By Ivor Beake

EVERY morning at eight o'clock, just as rush-hour is getting into full flood, Daisy Duck, of Upton Farm, waves a wing at the drivers and leads her brood across Belvedere Way to reach the pond just in front of the pub, the Dipping Inn.

There are eleven ducklings this year and each of them follow Daisy in single file as she waddles unceremoniously along.

Cars line up as far as the crossroads, hooting their horns and flashing their lights, but Daisy ignores them all. 'As far as Daisy's concerned,' says Evie Feathers, farmer's wife, 'getting across to that pond is the only thing that matters. The drivers can hoot and flash their lights as much as they like but it won't stop her!' Things are now so bad that the Council is erecting a sign to show that the ducks crossing have right of way.

Mr. Paul Thomas of Belvedere Close said, 'There's no other way round to the main road. I'm late for work every morning and my boss is getting fed up with the excuse. But what can I do?'

I asked Daisy could she perhaps think of making a later start – after the rush-hour? And her reply?

'Quack! Quack! Quack!' I take that as a No.

Term 2 Unit of work 9:

Compose an argument

Resource Book pages 22–25

Writing Objective:

T18: To construct effective arguments: developing a point logically and effectively; supporting and illustrating points persuasively; anticipating possible objections.

Links to Sentence/Word Level Work

S5: To ... investigate conditionals ... use these forms to construct sentences which express, e.g. possibilities, hypotheses.

Text Copymasters: C27–30

Discussing the Text:

- Explain the task to the children, which is to write a letter to the Council, arguing for a footbridge or footpath to the school.
- Discuss the prompt sheet on Resource Book page 25, 'Writing an argument.'
- Read together the text on pages 22–25, which is a letter to Editor of the Gazette. *What does the writer use to persuade the reader to his/her opinion. How does it begin?*
- Check on the children's knowledge of the features of a formal letter. *How do we write it?* It needs to be factual, not emotive, it needs to give reasons and be in formal polite language, particularly if we do not know the person.
- Explain that arguments may be introduced using if ... then, might, could, etc.

Shared Writing

Teacher Demonstration

- Make up a sender's and a recipient's address and write them.
- Reminding children how to begin a formal letter, compose and write an opening paragraph. (See Shared Writing Example opposite.)

Teacher Scribing

- Keeping the prompt sheet and text model on display if possible, take suggestions from the children for how the letter will proceed.
- Discuss ideas putting points for the case, allow the children to verbalise them for the letter, and scribe them.

Supported Composition

- In pairs, children discuss, rehearse and write the concluding parts of the letter.
- Check and compare.

Independent Writing

- Using the prompt sheet and the model text to help them, children to write a letter to the editor of the classroom newspaper *Issues*. Allow the children to chooose whether to put the case *for* or *against* walking to school.

Checking Children's Learning

- Can children describe to you the features of writing an argument?
- Can children tell you why it is important to put the points in a logical order?

Revisiting the Objective

- Write a reply from the Council, objecting to the children's proposal.

Shared Writing Example:

Class 6Y
Edgehill Primary
School
Lower Edgehill
Walkwood
Leics. WA3 4BW

The Director
Town Council Office
Upper Edgehill
Walkwood
Leics. WA3 1HQ

Dear Sir

Would you please consider a request for the construction of a fenced footpath from and across Edgehill Common to Edgehill School.

Our reasons for this request are simple. There are almost a hundred children at this school. The majority of us want to walk to school and back again. We are obliged to walk all around the common and then cross the main road through the village.

Firstly, you will be aware that with the new out of town supermarket, at the south end of the village, traffic is much greater than it has ever been before so there is an issue of safety.

Secondly, there is a time factor. If a fenced footpath could be constructed straight across the common, it would cut some fifteen minutes off most journeys. This saving of half an hour a day may not seem much but would be a huge help on dark mornings and winter afternoons. Also, many children would be able to walk unsupervised whereas, now, their parents dare not let them.

We appreciate that older villagers may object because it would mean change but we feel they would soon begin to see the benefits for themselves. We also realise that it would cost the council money, but it would be such a help for the villagers and their children that it would be worth it.

Please consider our plan because, in the long run, a fenced footpath can only help to modernise our village and, by allowing us to walk to school, be of benefit to our future health.

Yours faithfully,

Term 2 Unit of work 10:

Present a formal argument

Resource Book pages 26–27

Writing Objective:
T18: To construct effective arguments: developing a point logically and effectively; tailoring the writing to formal presentation where appropriate.

Text Copymasters: C31–32

Discussing the Text:

- Explain the task to the children, which is (Session 1) to *plan and make notes* of arguments for *and* against the use of mobile phones in school, in order to (Session 2) *write a formal letter* to the Director of Education putting the case *against* them.
- Read through the text on Resource Book pages 26 and 27, 'Mobile Phones for Children'.
- Discuss with the children further ideas they may come up with for and against the argument.

Shared Writing

Session 1
Teacher Demonstration

- Remind the children that, at this stage, you are writing notes only. *How do we write notes? Do we need proper sentences? Do we use abbreviations? How can we show which side of the argument the point needs to be noted?*
- Draw a vertical line and head one side 'For', one side 'Against'.
- Take an argument for each side from the text on pages 26 and 27 and write it in, using suggested short forms etc. (See Shared Writing Example 1, below.)

Teacher Scribing

- Take further points from the children until you have covered all possible arguments and scribed them.

Shared Writing Example 1:

For	***Against***
safety	easy to steal
always in touch	cause arguments
instant communication	disrupt lessons
can get help	instead of concentrating on work, pupils busy txt-messaging
if U have to stay at school U can let people know	cause envy
health hazard not proved	expensive to use
	health hazard
	irritate teachers
	stop others concentrating
	antisocial

Teacher Demonstration

- Show the children how they might prioritise the notes. First look at the points 'for' mobile phones in school. *How many points are there?* Six. *What's the most important point? We'll label it 1. What's the least important point? We'll label it 6. Out of the points left, which is most important? We'll label it 2. Which is least important? Label it 5.* Repeat until all are covered. Do the same with points against. *We do not have to include the points in this order but it gives us some idea of their relative importance.*
- Compose with the children the first two paragraphs of a formal letter to the Director of Education, putting the case *against* the use of mobile phones in school. Use a new argument in each paragraph. (See Example 2.)

Teacher Scribing

- Take suggestions for the next paragraph and scribe.

Supported Composition

- Ask children to write a paragraph giving another argument against mobiles, from the notes. Then share, select and scribe.
- Complete the letter together, scribing for the class.

Shared Writing Example 2:

Dear Sir

I am concerned about the use of mobile phones in school.

First and foremost are the health issues. Mobile phones have not yet been proved to be safe. We should be very cautious while children are developing and growing.

Mobiles cause disruption to lessons. Instead of concentrating on their work, pupils are often text messaging their friends. This stops other children from concentrating.

Mobiles are a great source of envy and jealousy; arguments frequently break out over them.

It is very irritating when mobiles ring or beep during lessons or when dozens of them are in use at breaktimes. The pupils who are busy on them are not socialising with the people they are physically with.

Mobiles are easy to steal and cause a lot of trouble, as well as being expensive to use. My feeling is that they should be banned from schools.

Yours faithfully

Independent Writing

- Children to write another letter to the Director of Education, putting the case *for* mobile phones in school.

Checking Children's Learning

- Can the children tell you the steps in planning a constructive argument?

Revisiting the Objective

- Brainstorm another issue and construct arguments for and against.

Term 2 Unit of work 11:

Write a balanced report

Resource Book pages 28–31

Writing Objective:
T19: To write a balanced report of a controversial issue: summarising fairly the competing views; analysing strengths and weaknesses of different positions.

Text Copymasters: C33–36

Discussing the Text:

- Read and discuss Resource Book page 31, 'Writing a Balanced Report'. *What might a 'balanced report' be?*
- Read the text 'Meat Eating Versus Vegetarianism' on pages 28 to 30. *Is this 'balanced'? What makes it balanced? How does this text tie in with the features listed on page 31?*
- Go through the prompt sheet again, comparing the text to see how far its features have been followed.
- Explain the task to the children, which is (Session 1) to note points for and against mobile phones in general, and (Session 2) to write an opening for a balanced report on them for the classroom newspaper *Issues*.

Supported Composition

- In pairs the children write their own notes for and against mobile phones using strategies learned in the previous session.
- Check and compare.
- Choose one set of notes, scribe and read through them together.

Shared Writing Example 1:

For	***Against***
safety	easy to steal
always in touch	disruptive
instant communication	irritating
can get help	expensive to use
can let people know if you are delayed	health hazard
health hazard not proved	irritate others
modern communication	stop others concentrating
can save lots of time	antisocial
useful in a crisis or accident	batteries run out quickly

Session 2
Teacher Demonstration

- Referring back to the Prompt Sheet, compose and write an opening paragraph for a balanced report on mobile phones. (See Shared Writing Example 2.)

Supported Composition

- Using the prompt sheet on page 31 and the Vegetarian text (pages 28 to 30) as a model, children write the next paragraph.

Shared Writing Example 2:

Mobile phones are a modern, up-to-date method of communication which many people really like, though others find them a disruption and an irritant.

With a mobile you are always in touch, you can let others know where you are and that you are safe. You have instant communication, though other people sometimes think that this can be a nuisance in classrooms or on trains and buses.

Some people think that mobiles might be a health hazard but this has not yet been proved. They also say that they are antisocial, but that all depends upon the person who is using it!

Mobiles are invaluable for saving time when an accident or crisis has happened, help can be with you right away, though some people criticise the fact that they have a short battery life and say, 'It's always run out when you need it!'

Mobile phones are probably here to stay, whether you like them or not, and the hope is that the next generation of mobiles will have conquered all the faults and developed in a way that makes them only useful.

Independent Writing

- Children finish writing their own balanced report.

Checking Children's Learning

- Can the children tell you what a 'balanced report' is?
- Can the children tell you the features to keep in mind when writing a balanced report?

Revisiting the Objective

- Using the prompt sheet and previous work, write a balanced report on the issue of walking to school.

NB: Keep your Shared Writing from Session 2 for possible use after the end of Unit 12.

Term 2 Unit of work 12:

Summarise an argument

Resource Book pages 28–31

Writing Objective:
S4: To revise work on contracting sentences: summary.

Text Copymaster:

Discussing the Text:

- Check the children's understanding of summary writing. *The idea is to reduce the number of words. We can do this by changing the sentences, making them smaller – contracting them – or putting them together, not just by leaving words out.*
- Explain the task, which is to make a summary of the text 'Meat Eating Versus Vegetarianism' on Resource Book pages 28 to 30, losing a third of the number of words. *If we aim to contract every sentence or paragraph by about a third we will be left with two thirds of the original text.*

Shared Writing

Teacher Demonstration

- Read through the introduction with the children – page 28, paragraph 1. Aim to reduce it by about five words, by paraphrasing it.
- Compose and write. (See Shared Writing Example 1.)
- Repeat the process with the next paragraph on page 28. (See Example.)

Shared Writing Exampleb 1:

p 28, paragraph 1
Many people, for many reasons, are giving up meat. Why?

p 28, paragraph 2
A vegetarian diet may be healthier in having less fat, but meat is an important source of essential protein.

Teacher Scribing

- Turn over to page 29 and take suggestions from the children for paraphrasing the next two paragraphs, and scribe them. (See Example 2, below.)

Shared Writing Example:

p 29, paragraph 1
People worry about animal diseases like BSE and scrapie being transferred to humans, but the link has yet to be proved.

p 29, paragraph 2
Vegetarians are concerned with animal welfare, objecting to animals being kept in confined spaces and force fed, but strict government rules about this protect animals from cruelty.

Supported Composition

- In pairs, children read the final two paragraphs (page 30). They discuss and then write their suggestions for summarising the text.
- Check and compare. (See Shared Writing Example 3.)

Shared Writing Example 3:

p 30, paragraph 1

It may be wasteful to grow animal feeding crops rather than eat the plants (peas, beans, cereal) ourselves but meat eaters are convinced that modern farming provides us all with a healthy diet.

p 30, paragraph 2

People must make their own choice, keeping the welfare of both humans and animals in mind.

Independent Writing

- Give the children part, or all, of the text on Resource Book pages 18 to 21 ('Dry Earth – Deserts') to summarise.

Checking Children's Learning

- Can the children explain what a summary is?
- Can the children tell you how to contract sentences?

Revisiting the Objective

- Write a summary of the balanced report on mobile phones written in Unit 11.

Term 2 Unit of work 13:

Make notes 'for' and 'against'

Resource Book pages 22–24

Writing Objective:
S4: To revise work on contracting sentences for note making.

Text Copymasters: C27–29

Discussing the Text:

- Reread together the text on Resource Book pages 22 to 24, Letter to the Editor.
- Explain the task to the children, which is to make notes from the text, giving the arguments *for* walking.
- Recap on how to make notes from the text: *We can contract sentences, we can extract phrases, we can use abbreviations, etc. We need to find the important bit of the sentence, the bit that is telling us something, and we can lose the rest of it.*

Shared Writing

Teacher Demonstration

- Read the first sentence aloud (see Resource Book page 22), compose and write the first note. (Shared Writing Example 1)

Shared Writing Example: 1

p 22, paragraph 1
one alternative to traffic congestion – walking

Teacher Scribing

- Reminding the children how to extract the important bit of the sentence, take suggestions from them for making notes on the contents of the rest of pages 22 and 23, sentence by sentence. (See Shared Writing Example 2.)

Supported Composition

- The children make notes on the remaining paragraphs, one sentence at a time.
- Check each sentence and compare.

Shared Writing Example:

p 22, paragraph 2

we've 2 legs + 2 feet

why not use them as transport?

p 23, paragraph 1

many arguments 4 wlkg

wlkg quicker

overtake rush hour cars, take short cuts

p 23, paragraph 2

healthier

wlkg, 1 of best forms exercise

many overweight chn, too little exercise

wlkg to school, ideal exercise

p 23, paragraph 3

town less stressful, quiet, clean, less polluting cars

p 23, paragraph 4

wlkg is free

p 24, paragraph 1

when time, should try

wlk to work/school/shops once/twice week 2 see difference

Independent Writing

- Choose one of the articles written *against* walking to school for the classroom *Issues* news magazine, and make notes from it.

Checking Children's Learning

- Can the children tell you what it means to 'contract sentences'?
- Can the children tell you features of note-making?

Revisiting the Objective

- Use the non-chronological report text on Resource Book pages 18 to 21, 'Dry Earth – Deserts', to make notes in the same way.

Term 2 Unit of work 14:

Make a contract

Resource Book pages 32–33

Writing Objective:

T20: To discuss the way standard English varies in different contexts, e.g. why legal language is ... highly formalised.

Text Copymasters: C37–38

Discussing the Text:

- Read through and discuss the meanings of the Confusing Notices on Resource Book page 32. *What is wrong with these?* They are ambiguous, they are not clear, they are confusing. Discuss how ambiguity arises, and ask children for examples of the language that has confused them. *It is very easy to write in an ambiguous manner, we have to be very critical of our own writing and work out ways of saying things that leave no space for argument or confusion. To avoid ambiguity we have to write in a way that is specific, clear and precise.*
- Read the text on page 33, 'Making a Contract'. *This is a contract for pocket money. What's wrong with it?* It needs to show who's making the contract, whose pocket money is going to be increased, when, by how much and precisely what for. It should show how many times the jobs have to be done and how the parties to the contract will know they are done to an acceptable level.
- Explain the task to the children, which is (Session 1) to rewrite the pocket money contract to eliminate all vague areas and (Session 2, page 38) to write a homework contract along the same lines.

Shared Writing

Session 1
Teacher Demonstration

- Read through the contract again with the children, identifying and annotating all the parts which are ambiguous or open to argument. (See Shared Writing Example 1.)

Teacher Scribing

- Take suggestions from the children for rewriting the contract, making precise all the parts previously identified as vague. (See Shared Writing Example 2.)
- Check that all parts of your new contract are unambiguous.

Shared Writing Example 1:

Who is making this contract?
In return for increasing your pocket money, you will have to do more jobs.
whose?
by how much?
Which jobs exactly?
How many times?
To what standard?

Shared Writing Example 2:

Pocket Money Contract between
Mr. & Mrs. D. Robinson and David Robinson

We, Mr. & Mrs. D. Robinson, agree to raise the pocket money of David Robinson to £5.00 per week from the date of this contract, in return for which he will be expected to add the following to his list of chores:

- Make own bed every morning – properly, not just straightened
- Walk dog around block every day after school
- Put football kit into washing machine immediately after playing, every time. (Forfeit 50p every time it's left in kit bag)
- Remove all boots, trainers, running shoes etc. in porch and stack tidily when returning home; knock all mud into bin when dry, keep porch mud-free at all times

Signed: ....
(Parents)

....
(Child)

Date: ....

Session 2
Teacher Demonstration

- Reminding the children that the contract is to be precise, talk about what is needed in a homework contract – e.g. obligations on both sides, the children to *do* the homework, the teacher to *set and mark* the homework, all within given times – then compose and write together the introductory lines. (See Shared Writing Example 3.)

Supported Composition

- Using the pocket money contract as a model, give the children Time Out to discuss and write the first sentence of the homework contract. They may need to negotiate with you (See Example 3).

Shared Writing Example 3:

Homework Contract
between Ms. D. James and the children of class 6D

This Homework Contract gives the obligations of all parties and, as such, is understood and signed by them.

Ms. D. James agrees to:

- Set weekly homework in accordance with curriculum and children's needs.
- Collect in homework on the first school day of each week, mark it and return it with comments by the last school day of each week.

The pupils of class 6D agree to:

- Make notes of all homework activities when asked to
- Take home homework on the first school day of each week
- Return the completed homework within three days of collection
- Use teacher's marking and comments to improve future work.

Signed: ....
(Teacher)

....
(Child)

Date: ....

Independent Writing

- Children complete the homework contract.

Checking Children's Learning

- Can the children give you verbal examples of ambiguous language?
- Can the children explain why ambiguity arises?
- Can the children tell you how to avoid ambiguity in writing?

Revisiting the Objective

- Find some different pieces of text – pamphlets, instructions, legal advice etc. – and discuss the reasons for the different ways the language is written.

Term 2 Unit of work 15:

Write a questionnaire

Resource Book page 34

Writing Objective:
T20: To discuss the way standard English varies in different contexts, why questionnaires must be specific.

Text Copymaster: C39

Discussing the Text:

- Recap with the children on the formality of legal language, from the last session. Then talk about questionnaires, how they are written in a formal way, but not a legal way, in order to prompt responses that will give enough information for a survey to be worthwhile. *What questionnaires have you seen? What was their purpose?*
- Ask the children what they think the features of a good questionnaire might be.
- Read through the text on Resource Book page 34, 'Television Watching Survey'. *How far does this questionnaire fit our suggested pattern? How specific is it? Could we make it more specific?*
- *What is the purpose of the questionnaire? How do we know who is going to answer it in a household?*
- Explain the task to the children, which is to rewrite the questionnaire to make it more specific. *We need to go through it carefully, jotting down notes where we think we could make it better. In some places it might be better to use tick boxes so that people have a choice of responses.* Explain how tick boxes work.

Shared Writing

Teacher Scribing

- Clip the acetate sheet to Resource Book page 34 and annotate the text, making suggestions yourself and taking suggestions from the children. (See Shared Writing Example 1.)

Shared Writing Example 1:

TELEVISION WATCHING SURVEY

Need to establish size of household, age of occupants

- How many TV sets are there in your house?

- How much TV do you watch?

  each week or each night?
  1-10 hrs, 11-20 hrs, 21-30 hrs, 30+ hrs

  A separate question for weekends?

- What is your favourite kind of programme?

  ☐ sport ☐ films ☐ news
  ☐ soaps ☐ drama ☐ game shows

- What is your favourite programme?

- Do you have a video recorder?

  How many programmes do you record in a week?
  ☐ 1-3 ☐ 4-6 ☐ 6-10 ☐ 10+
  Do people watch all the recordings they have made?

- Who is your favourite person on TV?

- ~~What would you like more of?~~

  Give three programmes or types of programme that you would like to see more of on TV.

TELEVISION WATCHING SURVEY

Number of people who live in your house: ________

Age of occupants, state how many of each age in each box

☐ over 50 ☐ 40–50 ☐ 20–40 ☐ 10–20 ☐ 0–10

State number of TV sets in your house. ______

How much TV do you watch each week?

☐ 1–10 hrs ☐ 11–20 hrs ☐ 21–30 hrs ☐ 30+ hrs

How much television do you watch on Saturdays and Sundays?

☐ less than 3 hrs ☐ 3–8 hrs ☐ 10+ hrs

Tick your favourite kind of programme

☐ sport ☐ films ☐ news

☐ soaps ☐ drama ☐ gameshows

What is your favourite programme? ________________________

Do you have a video recorder? ☐ Yes ☐ No

How many programmes do you record in a week?

☐ 1–3 ☐ 4–6 ☐ 6–10 ☐ more than 10

How many of the recorded programmes do you find time to watch?

____

Who is your favourite person on TV?

____

Give three programmes or types of programme that you would like to see more of on TV.

____

____

Independent Writing

- Children write out the changed questionnaire, adding more questions if they wish to. (See Shared Writing Example 2.)

Checking Children's Learning

- Can the children explain how the purpose of the questionnaire will influence how it is written?
- Can the children tell you one way of making questions more specific?

Revisiting the Objective

- Use Copymaster C4 to rewrite the questionnaire for a survey on Pets to make it specific.

Term 3 Unit of work 16:

Divide text into paragraphs

Resource Book page 35

Writing Objective:

T21: To divide whole texts into paragraphs, paying attention to the sequence of paragraphs and to the links between one paragraph and the next, e.g. through the choice of appropriate connectives.

Text Copymaster: C40

Discussing the Text:

- Introduce the concept of paragraphs and check the children's knowledge.
- Read through the prompt sheet 'Writing Paragraphs' on Resource Book page 35 together and discuss its information.
- Read through the text on Copymaster C5, which is a Year 6 pupil's report on The Olympic Games.
- Discuss the fact that it is written as one whole paragraph. *Is this right or not? Why?*

Shared Writing

Teacher Scribing

- Keeping the prompt sheet in mind, use the acetate to annotate the text.
- Take children's suggestions and write directions to show where new paragraphs might begin and where linking connectives can be used. Edit the text for repetition, clarity and coherence at the same time.

Shared Writing Example:

The Olympic Games

The Olympic Games started in Ancient Greece. They were held every four years and they still are today. (new para) In ancient days if there was a war ~~the war~~ it was stopped to let the games take place. In modern times no games were held in 1916, 1940 and 1944 because of the First World War and the Second World War. (new para) In ancient ~~days~~ times, all the games were held in Olympia in Greece and only Greek people and people from Mediterranean countries were allowed to enter. Today, a different city hosts the games each time and people from all over the world compete. The stadium in Olympia is still there now and it is very small, nothing like the huge places where the games are held nowadays. (new para) ~~Only~~ Originally, only men could enter but now women compete and win the same honours as men. (new para) The games have changed in some ways. One of the most popular events today is the Marathon which did not exist in the early games. We also have winter games now, which are held in the same year as the summer games. (new para) However Ancient Greece was much too hot for winter sports like tobogganing and ice hockey.

Shared Writing Example: edited piece

The Olympic Games

The Olympic Games started in Ancient Greece. They were held every four years and they still are today.

In ancient days if there was a war the war was stopped to let the games take place. In modern times no games were held in 1916, 1940 and 1944 because of the First World War and the Second World War.

In ancient times all the games were held in Olympia in Greece and only Greek people and people from Mediterranean countries were allowed to enter. Today, a different city hosts the games each time and people from all over the world compete. The stadium in Olympia is still there now and it is very small, nothing like the huge places where the games are held nowadays.

Originally, only men could enter but now women compete and win the same honours as men.

The games have changed in some ways. One of the most popular events today is the Marathon, which did not exist in the early games. We also have winter games now, which are held in the same year as the summer games.

However, Ancient Greece was much too hot for winter sports like tobogganing and ice hockey.

Supported Composition

- Give the children Time Out, in pairs, to annotate the first half of the text on Copymaster C6, Helen of Troy, together and then edit it.

Independent Writing

- Children complete the second half of the text.

Checking Children's Learning

- Can the children tell you the main features of a paragraph?
- Can the children tell you two ways of showing a new paragraph in their writing?

Revisiting the Objective

- Choose a child's text to edit and put into paragraphs.

Term 3 Unit of work 17:

Write notices

Resource Book pages 36–37

Writing Objective:

S3: To revise formal styles of writing: the impersonal voice; the use of the passive.

Text Copymasters: C41–42

Discussing the Text:

- Check the children's knowledge of 'active' and 'passive' voice. *What does it mean if we write in the passive?* The subject and the object of the verb change places, so instead of saying (e.g.) 'the dog bit Jack' we say 'Jack *was bitten* by the dog'; instead of 'The monster ate the alien' we say 'the alien *was eaten* by the monster'.
- Read through the texts on Resource Book pages 36 to 37 'Public Notices'.
- Explain that these notices are all written in the active voice, as commands or instructions. *We are going to change them into the passive voice.* Public notices are often written in the passive.

Shared Writing

Teacher Demonstration

- Clip the acetate over pages 36–37, or use a flip chart.
- Keeping the examples in mind, verbalising as you are composing, rewrite the first notice, e.g. *What is banned? Swimming. We write that first as the subject. We can write 'Swimming in the lake is banned/not allowed/forbidden! I will put 'forbidden' which sounds like a formal notice.*
- Repeat with the second notice (See Shared Writing Example, opposite.).

Teacher Scribing

- Take suggestions from the children for changing the next four active commands. You may find it helpful to underline the object of each notice in the Resource Book. When you rewrite the notice, the object becomes the subject in each case.
- Check whether children identify the ambiguity in the sixth example (it might mean that you have to carry a dog if you go on the escalator!)

Supported Composition

- Give the children Time Out in pairs to verbalise and then write the next two notices.
- Check and compare.

Shared Writing Example:

p 36

No swimming in the lake

Swimming in the lake is forbidden

Keep dogs on the lead at all times

Dogs must be kept on the lead at all times

Keep off the grass

This grass must not be walked on

No smoking

Smoking is not allowed

Wash your hands before cooking

Hands must be washed before cooking

p 37

Carry dogs on the escalator

Dogs must be carried on the escalator.

Cleaning in progress

This room is being cleaned

Do not sunbathe on this beach with no clothes on

Nude sunbathing on this beach is banned

Do not drive on the motor way with a bag on your head

Driving on the motorway with a bag on your head is forbidden

Wear a seat belt on all journeys

Seat belts should be worn on all journeys

Independent Writing

Children rewrite the last two notices in the passive.

Checking Children's Learning

Can the children explain the difference between the active and passive voice?
Can the children give you verbal examples of each?

Revisiting the Objective

Brainstorm some more active commands, then change them to the passive voice.

Term 3 Unit of work 18:

Write an explanation

Resource Book pages 38–39

Writing Objective:

T20: To secure control of impersonal writing, particularly the sustained use of the present tense and the passive voice, and use of complex sentences.

Links to Sentence/Word Level Work

S3: To revise formal styles of writing: the impersonal voice; the use of the passive.

Text Copymasters: C43–44

Discussing the Text:

- Clip the acetate to Resource Book pages 38 and 39.
- Read together the text 'How Wool Yarn is Made'.
- *What kind of text is this?* It is an explanation text.
- *What features of the text can we identify? How is it different from, say, a letter to a friend?* It is written in an impersonal way, in the passive voice.
- Look for examples of the passive voice. Underline them (See Shared Writing Example 1).
- Explain the task, which is to write a similar text, using this as a model.

Shared Writing Example 1:

Wool yarn is made by pulling fleece into strips. Then the strips are twisted to make them stay together and make them strong.

The twisting process that makes yarn is called spinning. Spinning has been done by hand for over 2,000 years. Some people still spin by hand, but today most wool yarn is spun on machines. Almost any kind of hair can be spun, but the most common is sheep's wool.

Two or more different fibres can be mixed together before being spun into a single yarn. This is called a blended yarn.

Shared Writing

Teacher Demonstration

- Choose a topic that the children are studying elsewhere in the curriculum.
- If necessary, make notes of information on a flip chart first.
- Write an introductory paragraph using an impersonal and passive style.

Teacher Scribing

- Again remind the children of the passive voice, and take suggestions from them for a paragraph of information, and scribe it. (See Shared Writing Example 2)

Supported Composition

- In pairs, children write a further paragraph.
- Check and compare, making sure they are sustaining the impersonal tone of the piece.

Shared Writing Example 2:

Lakes

Lakes are bodies of water which are found inland. They are formed in depressions in the land. These depressions are known as 'basins'.

Rainfall or melting snow can make a flow of water into low areas. This water gets into the lake basin through brooks, streams, rivers and underground springs.

Lake basins can be formed in different ways. They may be formed when the earth's crust warps or develops a fault, or by volcanoes or glaciers. Silt and mud may be deposited when a river overflows and when the tributary valleys are flooded a lake may form.

There are many lakes, all over the world. Lake Superior in North America was created by an earth fault. The other Great Lakes were created by glaciers.

Independent Writing

- Children write a conclusion to the text.

Checking Children's Learning

- Can the children tell you how an impersonal voice is sustained?
- Can the children write a brief explanation of how something is made, showing the use of the passive?

Revisiting the Objective

- Choose another topic which the children know about and repeat the process.

Term 3 Unit of work 19:

Identify text types

Resource Book pages 40–47

Writing Objective:
T22: To select the appropriate style and form to suit a specific purpose and audience, drawing on knowledge of different non-fiction text types.

Text Copymasters: C45–53

Discussing the Text:

- Recap on some of the different kinds of texts and forms that the children have worked on.
- Read together the table on Resource Book pages 40 and 41, 'Writing in different styles and forms', discussing some recent texts read and where they might fit into it.
- Explain the tasks to the children which are (Session 1) to identify the type and features of example texts, and (Session 2) to look at some sample titles, decide where they might fit in the table and compose the openings for some of them.

Shared Writing

Session 1
Teacher Scribing

- Read together the text on Resource Book pages 42 and 43, 'Training your dog to 'sit''. *What are the features of this text? What kind of text is this?* It is an instruction text. Show the children that it will fit into row 4 of the table on pages 40 and 41.
- *What form does it take? For instance, is it a letter? A recipe? Part of a diary?* Ask the children to decide on its form, moving along row 4 until you come to the appropriate column (instruction leaflet). *Are we sure this is what it is?* When the children are certain, write the title in the appropriate box.
- Repeat this process with the text on pages 44–45, 'Little Greening Dog Show', drawing out that it is a newspaper report of *what happened* at the Dog Show, therefore it is a recount.

Supported Composition

- In pairs, children read the text on pages 46–47, 'Do you want your dog to suffocate?' and complete a box in the table for it.
- Check and compare.

Independent Writing

- Children read the last item, 'Dog Illnesses – Heat Stroke' and fill in the box accordingly.

Shared Writing Example:

TEXT TYPE	diary	newspaper report	wall display	Formal letter	informal letter	recipe	instruction leaflet	poster	leaflet
Recount		Little Greening Dog Show							
Explanation									
Report									
Instructions							Training your dog to 'sit'		
Persuasion								Do you want your dog to suffocate?	
Discussion									

Session 2
Teacher Scribing

- Remind the children that in this session you are going to look at some sample openings, decide where they might fit in, and compose openings for them.
- Scribe these three examples and take suggestions from the children for where they fit. *The Big Match: Arsenal Over the Moon*, *How to Tackle Your Opponent*, *Cheesy Footballs*.
- Recap on the features of writing a recipe. Take suggestions from the children for beginning the recipe for Cheesy Footballs.

Supported Composition

- In pairs, children discuss and then write the second part of the Cheesy Football recipe.

Shared Writing Example:

TEXT TYPE	diary	newspaper report	wall display	Formal letter
Recount		Arsenal over the Moon	Irish Dancing	
Explanation			How to Tackle Your Opponent	
Report				
Instructions				The New School Uniform
Persuasion				
Discussion				

informal letter	recipe	instruction leaflet	poster	leaflet
Dear Gran				
	Cheesy Footballs			

Dear Gran

You'll never guess what happened this week at school! You know that book you bought me by Wendy Body – well, she came to school this week and told us all about her writing life! And I knew she was coming so I took my book. Guess what! She signed it for me! And she wrote 'Keep writing, Tom – love from Wendy'. It was like just so brilliant ...

The New School Uniform

Dear parents,

This letter is to confirm that our new school uniform has now been decided. The pupils and the governors, with some parents, have agreed, and the new school uniform will be required clothing from the 2nd September.

It will consist of:

Green sweatshirt with the school logo
Yellow cotton polo shirt
Green trousers or joggers
Black shoes

The uniform will be available from ...

Independent Writing

- Children identify the style and form of two more samples, and write their beginnings, bearing in mind the features of the texts they are modelling.

Checking Children's Learning

- Can the children explain the difference between 'style' and 'form'?
- Can the children tell you why it is important to know the purpose and audience before beginning the writing?

Revisiting the Objective

- Collect some pieces of texts from various sources (leaflets, posters, flyers, letters, etc.). Identify their style and form and add to the matrix.

Term 3 Unit of work 20:

Select text type

Resource Book pages 40–48

Writing Objective:
T22: To select the appropriate style and form to suit a specific purpose and audience, drawing on knowledge of different non-fiction text types.

Text Copymasters: C45–53

Discussing the Text:

- Remind the children of the different styles and forms that they recapped on in the last two sessions.
- *Why is it important to know purpose and audience? What difference does knowing these factors make to our writing?* We can structure our writing style and language for our purpose and our audience.
- Explain the task to the children, which is to select a text type and form for a given purpose and audience, to devise a title and to write an appropriate opening.
- Go through the table on Resource Book pages 40 and 41 to select a text type and a form. For example, you might decide to write instructions for a younger class who are going to look after a hamster in the classroom. *Our audience is a Year 3 class. Our type of text is instructions, and our form is an instruction leaflet.*
  Give the children a suggested title, e.g. 'How to clean out Hamsterdam'.

Shared Writing

Session1
Teacher Scribing

- Prompted by the children, write the text (using Shared Writing Example 1 as required).
- Take suggestions from the children for other titles and scribe them.
- Run through all the ideas the children have for the instructions, scribing them on post-it notes.
- Make sure that all the children have all the information, and that they understand the task before they begin to write, by taking their ideas and scribing the features of instructional texts before the next activity.

Supported Composition

- In pairs, children write the opening sentences of the instructions.

Session 2
Teacher Scribing

- Take suggestions for further types of text, form, purpose and audience and scribe them. (See Shared Writing Example 2.)

Supported Composition

- In pairs, children choose what they will write and the purpose and decide on a title.
- Share titles, write opening sentences in pairs.

Shared Writing Example 1:

Type of text: instructions
Form: instructional leaflet
Audience: year 3 class

Title: **How to Clean out Hamsterdam.**

To keep the hamster clean and healthy you will need to clean his cage out regularly, at least once a week, preferably twice.

What you need:

- A bin bag for the rubbish
- A hard brush
- Soapy water and a cloth for cleaning dishes
- Clean newspaper
- A box to keep the hamster safe in
- Clean straw, sawdust and/or wood chippings

What you do:

1. Make sure the hamster is safe in his spare box.
2. Empty the cage of all rubbish.

Shared Writing Example 2:

Type of text: recount
Form: report
Audience: Head Teacher, Governors, Staff, Parents, Pupils of the school

Title: **Boys of Class 6X Save the Day**

On Tuesday of last week there was an emergency in the school when the boys' toilets flooded.
It happened at lunchtime. Two of the boys from class 6X went into the toilets and found that the washbays were full of water. Instead of panicking, the boys considered what they should do.

Independent Writing

- Children to finish, individually, the piece of text chosen for the supported composition.

Checking Children's Learning

- Can the children tell you at least seven different types of text?
- Can the children tell you at least ten different forms?

Revisiting the Objective

Brainstorm a completely different set of factors and repeat the process.

CURRICULUM VITAE

Name: ______________________________

Address:

____

____

____

____

Date of birth: ______________ Place of birth: ______________

Education

Employment

Roald Dahl's schooldays

Dahl says himself that he was always an outsider, he never behaved as people expected him to.

His handwriting was always messy.

Every summer the family travelled to Norway, where his grandmother told him stories about witches, giants and magic.

When he was first sent to school, Dahl was very homesick. He pretended to be ill and was sent home. His GP soon saw through him and sent him back to school, but never told his secret to anyone, pretending he had given him something to make him better. In return, Dahl promised not to play such a trick again.

Dahl was bullied at school by both his peers and the teachers.

He was beaten for making mistakes and talking in class.

Dahl was very good at sport – cricket, gold, football, hockey, and was captain of the squash team.

He won a boxing championship.

When he left school at 18, he was desperate to travel, so he joined Shell Oil.

School report

C3

Half-termly report from:

Name: ....

Year: ....

Term: ....

Subject	Comment	Grade
English:		
Maths:		
Latin:		
French:		
Geography:		
History:		
Science:		
Physical education:		
Conduct:		

Term ends on:

Signed:

Pets Survey

C4

How many pets have you got?

What sort of pets are they?

Who feeds them?

What do you feed them on?

Who keeps them clean or cleans their homes out?

Why do you like pets?

Are pets a good idea for everybody?

Which is your favourite pet?

Which pet is most popular in your class?

How many people hove pets in your school?

What are they?

What's good about having pets?

The Olympic Games started in Ancient Greece. They were held every four years and they still are today. In ancient days if there was a war the war was stopped to let the games take place. In modern times no games were held in 1916, 1940 and 1944 because of the First World War and the Second World War. In ancient days all the games were held in Olympia in Greece and only Greek people and people from Mediterranean countries were allowed to enter. Today, a different city hosts the games each time and people from all over the world compete. The stadium in Olympia is still there now and it is very small, nothing like the huge places where the games are held nowadays. Only men could enter but now women compete and win the same honours as men. One of the most popular events today is the Marathon. We also have winter games now, which are held in the same year as the summer games. Ancient Greece was much to hot for winter sports like tobogganing and ice hockey.

Helen of Troy

C6

One of the great myths of Ancient Greece is the story of Helen of Troy. Her mother was a human called Leda. Her father was the great God, Zeus. Everyone who saw Helen was dazzled by her beauty and all the princes in Sparta wanted to marry her. Her stepfather, the King of Sparta, said she must marry Menelaus and that everyone must be loyal to him. Menelaus eventually became the Spartan king. There was a Goddess of love, Aphrodite, and she promised Paris, a prince of Troy, that he would marry the most beautiful woman in the world. When Paris saw Helen he fell in love with her and she ran away with him. Menelaus started a war between the Spartans and the Trojans. The war happened in about 1200BC. Troy was destroyed. Helen went back to Sparta and her husband forgave her but legend says that she was later banished to the island of Rhodes.

Samuel Pepys – some facts about his life

1633 Born February 23rd

1648 Witnessed the execution of Charles I

1655 December – married Elizabeth Marchant de Saint Michel

1659 Became a clerk at the Exchequer

1660 *January 1st* Began writing his diary "Dined at home where my wife dressed the remains of a turkey and in the doing of it burned her hand" Also "my wife used to make coal fires and wash my foul clothes with her own hand..."

May Sailed with the fleet that brought back Charles II from exile.

November "Mr Fox came in … and then did take my wife and I to the Queen's presence chamber, where he got my wife placed behind the Queen's chaire."

Units of work 1 and 2

1661 Samuel and his wife attended the coronation of Charles II.

1662 Samuel learnt the multiplication tables. His wife and her maids ruled books for him to write in.

1664 *June 11th* "With my wife only to take the ayre, it being very warm and pleasant, … and thence to Hackney. Played at shuffleboard, ate cream and good cherries"

1665 The plague comes to the City of London.

1666 *September* The Great Fire of London.

1669 Samuel gave up keeping a diary because of his poor eyesight.

1703 *May 26th* Samuel Pepys died.

Units of work 1 and 2

Samuel Pepys and the Great Plague of 1665

Samuel Pepys (1633–1703) kept a diary between 1660 and 1669.

July 13th 1665: Above 700 died of the plague this week.

30th: It was a sad noise to hear our bell to toll and ring so often today, either for death or burials.

August 10th: By and by to the office ... in great trouble to see the Bill[1] this week rise so high ... above 3000 of the plague.

1 the Bill of Mortality, published every week, listed how many people had died in each parish

Units of work 1 and 2

12th: The people die so, that now ... they ... carry the dead to be buried by day-light, the nights not sufficing to do it in.

15th: I met a dead corpse of the plague, in the narrow alley ...

31st: In the City died this week ... 6102 of the plague.

September 3rd (Lord's day)

Alderman Hooper told us of a saddler, who had buried all the rest of his children of the plague, and himself and wife now being shut up and in despair of escaping, did desire only to save the life of his little child; and so prevailed to have it received stark-naked into the arms of a friend, who brought it (having put it into fresh clothes) to Greenwich

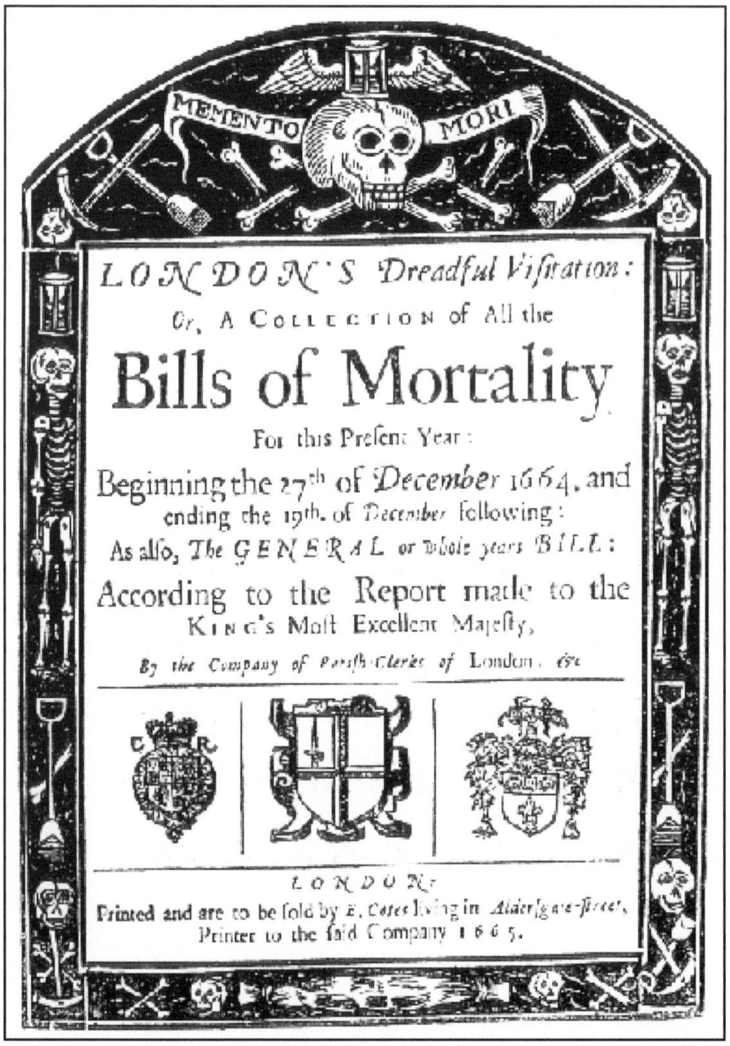

LONDON'S Dreadful Viſitation:
Or, A COLLECTION of All the
Bills of Mortality
For this Preſent Year:
Beginning the 27th of December 1664. and
ending the 19th. of December following:
As alſo, The GENERAL or whole years BILL:
According to the Report made to the
KING'S Moſt Excellent Majeſty,
By the Company of Pariſh-Clerks of London, &c.

LONDON:
Printed and are to be ſold by E. Cotes living in Alderſgate-ſtreet,
Printer to the ſaid Company 1665.

Bill of Mortality from the Great Plague of 1665

Units of work 1 and 2

Writing a Biography

The purpose

- Inform others about all or part of a person's life

What to do

- Do some research first eg: books, Internet or interview
- Write in the order in which events happened (chronological) – usually
- Describe important events in the person's life
- Give facts and opinions

How to write it

- Use the third person: 'he' or 'she'
- Use mainly past tense
- Use connecting clauses like 'After she left school,' or 'When she had finished college'. Avoid 'and then'.

Units of work 1 and 2

Roald Dahl

Roald Dahl was born in Wales of Norwegian parents. When he died in 1990 he was one of the best known of all children's authors. Despite the fantastic imagination that was to create Charlie and the Chocolate Factory and The BFG, Roald Dahl did not get on well at school: we know this from his autobiography – which was called 'Boy'.

Units of work 3 and 4

Dahl became a writer during the Second World War. He was a fighter pilot, even though he was so tall that he could hardly fit into the aeroplane's cockpit.

He shot down enemy planes, but he crashed and lived with bad backache and other aches and pains for the rest of his life.

He was posted to Washington, USA, in 1942 and met an American novelist who wanted ideas for flying stories. Dahl wrote some and the novelist, C. S. Forester, was so impressed that he had them published.

Later, Dahl wrote his children's stories in a little wooden shed in his garden at Gypsy House in Buckinghamshire. He fitted it out as a perfect den for writing in, and worked with a blanket around him when it was chilly.

Famous as he was, Dahl always cared about his readers. Quentin Blake, the illustrator, remembers how Dahl would sign books " ... though it might take two

Two different editions of *James and the Giant Peach*

Units of work 3 and 4

hours, everyone had a word and a signature" and how he would reply "... to thousands of letters with specially written poems...".

Dahl was married to the film actress Patricia Neale and they had four daughters and a son. One daughter, Olivia, died of measles when she was seven: in the 1960s children were not immunised against measles.

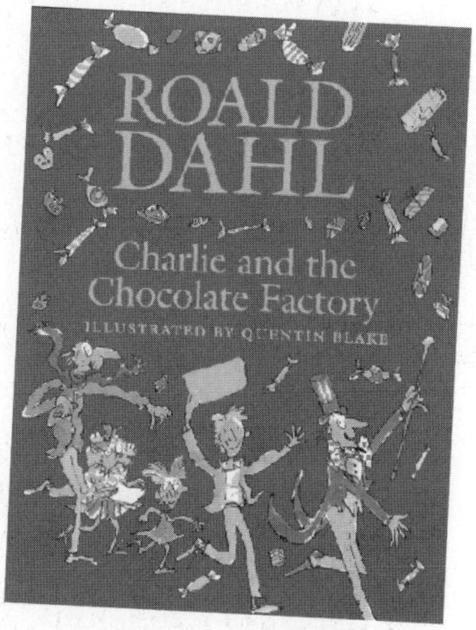

One of Roald Dahl's most famous stories is called *Charlie and the Chocolate Factory*.

Roald Dahl had both sadness and ill-fortune in his life along with happiness, so it is all the more remarkable that his writing has kept children laughing for years.

Danny and his dad from *Danny: Champion of the World*.

Units of work 3 and 4

Roald Dahl – A letter

Roald Dahl went to boarding school when he was nine. He wrote to his mother every week.

Dec 8th 1925

Dear Mama,

Just to make it a bit planer I will be coming home on December 17th, not the 18th. I will arrive a Cardiff a four o'clock please meet me, if that is not planer noufe let me know what you want to know about it.

Love from

Boy

Units of work 3 and 4

The fox cub that was saved by a PC's helmet

by Kate Ginn

EXHAUSTED and badly injured, the fox cub sought refuge in a rabbit hole as the frenzied pack of hounds moved in for the kill.

Huntsmen, bearing down ready to start digging out their quarry, clashed with hunt saboteurs who were attempting to block their way.

Death seemed to be just a matter of minutes away for the fox cowering inside the hole, until an extraordinary gesture from a policeman.

He took off his helmet so that it could be used by a saboteur to shield the entrance to the tunnel, to keep the snarling dogs at bay and save the animal's life.

While members of the Chidding-fold, Leconfield and Cowdray Hunt backed off, one of the anti-hunt protesters managed to rescue the terrified fox and, wrapping him up in a coat, took him away to safety.

DAILY MAIL, 16 FEBRUARY 1999

Journalistic writing

The purpose

- Inform the reader about topical issues in a lively and interesting way

What to do

- Devise a short, snappy, 'arresting' headline
- Include a by-line
- Grab the reader's attention with your opening sentence/paragraph and summarise what it's all about
- State the facts
  Remember: say *who, when, where, what, how* and *why*
- Report individuals' views and opinions

How to write it

- Make your sentences clear and concise
- Use direct or reported speech for eyewitness statements or people's opinions

Unit of work 6

Writing a report

The purpose

- Describe how things are (or were, for history).

What to do

- Start with a general opening statement about the subject
- State facts not opinions
- Write about things in a logical order eg: most important first
- You may use headings to group information
- Possibly use diagrams or illustrations

How to write it

- Use formal, impersonal language
- Use the third person eg: 'it' or 'they'
- Use present tense, except for historical reports
- You may use technical language related to the subject

Units of work 7 and 8

Dry Earth – Deserts

Deserts are places where it is dry nearly all the time.

Many, but not all, deserts are made from sand. Some deserts are made from rocks, pebbles and gravel. The North and South Poles are icy deserts.

About one fifth of the land in the world is desert land. This map shows where there are deserts.

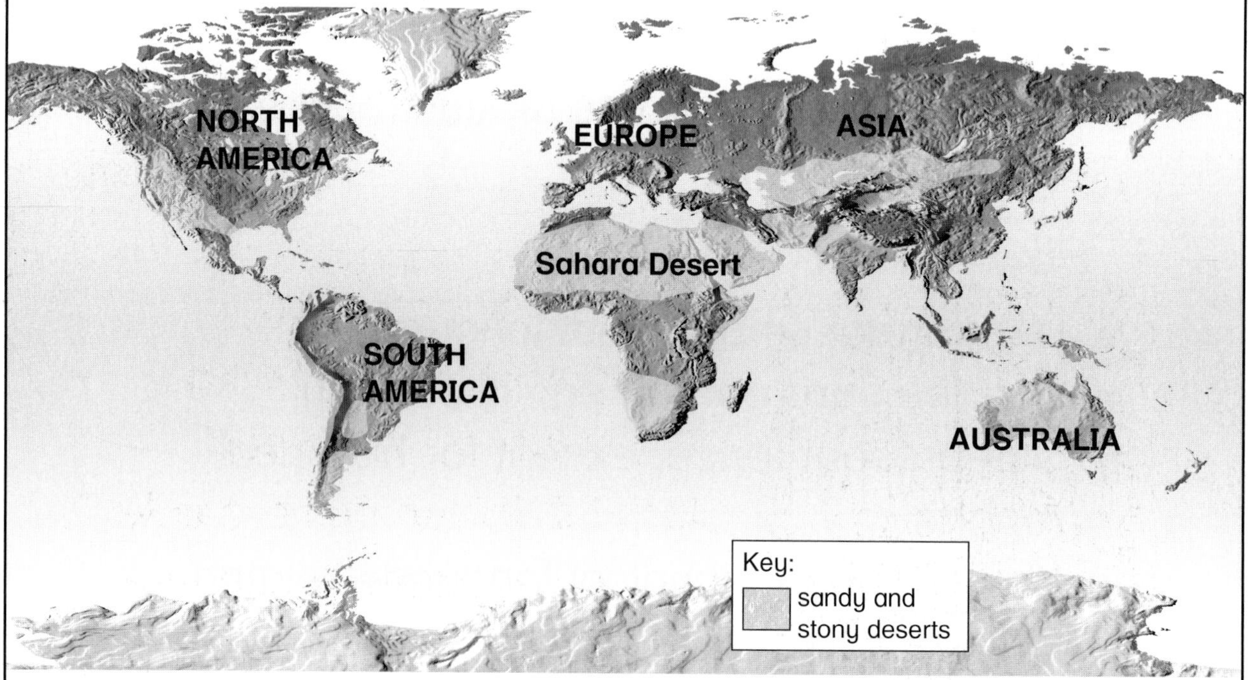

How can plants and animals survive in a desert?

Living things need water to survive. Yet less than 25cm of rain falls each year in a desert.

Plants and animals which can survive in deserts have special features which help them to find and / or save water.

Desert animals

Some *insects* which live in the desert have bodies with hard, waxy outer coverings, which help to conserve moisture. When it is too hot they shelter in tiny holes in rocks.

Darkling Beetle

Gila Monster

The *Gila Monster* is a poisonous lizard. It has a very thick tail which can store fat. When there is little food in the desert it can use this fat for energy. Its scaly skin helps it to save water.

Rattlesnakes have loose rings of skin at the ends of their tails. They rattle these rings to scare enemies. In the desert it is more sensible to rattle a tail than to hiss since hissing would use water.

Rattlesnake

Harris Hawk

Birds in the deserts are lucky because they can fly to search for water. Meat-eating birds like the Harris hawk do not need to find water for drinking. Instead they get their moisture from the animals they catch and eat.

Units of work 7 and 8

Camels have many features which help them to survive without food or water in the desert for many days.

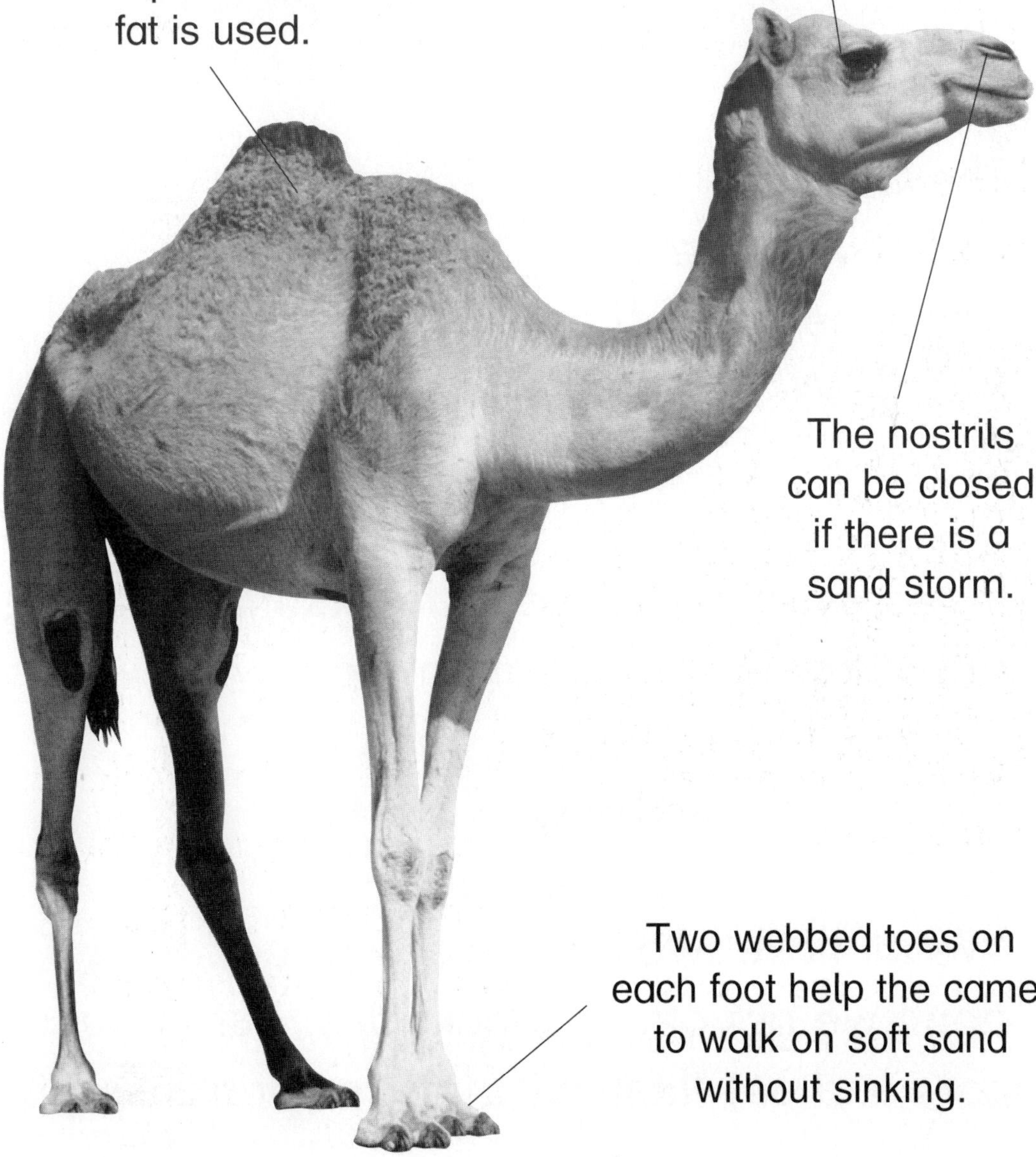

The hump stores fat. This can be used for energy. The hump shrinks as the fat is used.
Long eyelashes help to protect the eyes from sand and the Sun.
The nostrils can be closed if there is a sand storm.
Two webbed toes on each foot help the camel to walk on soft sand without sinking.

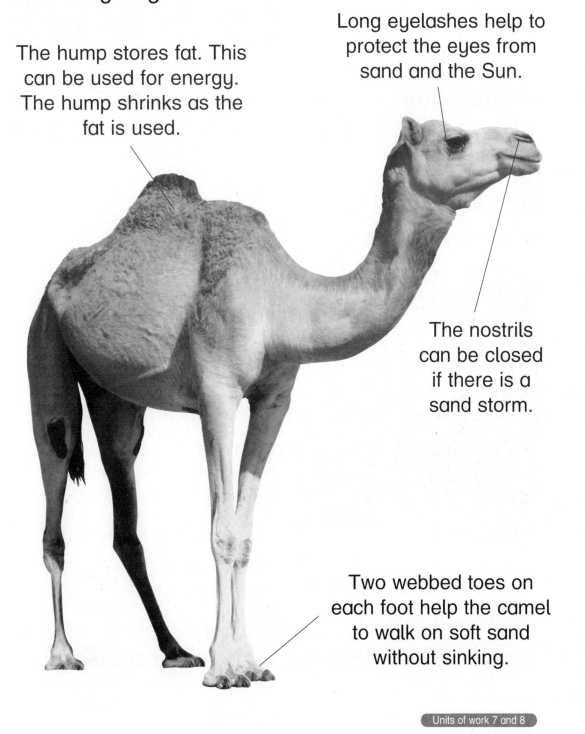

Units of work 7 and 8

54 Cromby Street
Ragstone
RS5 3TH

10th March

The Editor
The Gazette
Cromby House
Ragstone
RS5 3BW

Sir,
In response to the recent letters in the Rag about traffic congestion in the town, I would like to make a plea for one obvious alternative – walking!

We all have two legs and two feet. Why don't we get off our backsides, out of our cars and use them as a means of transport?

There are many arguments for walking. Firstly, it is often quicker. You can overtake cars in the rush hour and you can take short cuts on paths and side roads.

Secondly, it is healthier. Walking is one of the best forms of exercise. Recent reports have expressed concerns about the number of over-weight children and how few take regular exercise. Walking to school is an ideal way of getting exercise.

Other reasons which strengthen my case are to do with our general well-being. Think how much quieter, cleaner and less stressful our town would be with fewer polluting monsters on the road.

Last but not least in importance, walking is free.

I know people will say it's not practical for longer journeys and they haven't got the time, but I think we all ought to, at least, try it. So why don't we all agree to walk to work, to school or to the shops once or twice a week and see what a difference it makes to ourselves, our children and our environment?

Yours sincerely,

I. M. Walker (Mrs)

Writing an argument

The purpose

- Persuade someone to your point of view

What to do

- Introduce the issue and state your side of the argument in your first paragraph.
- Put the points for your case in order of importance.
- Support your case with evidence
- Deal with objections
- Summarise your points in the final paragraph

How to write it

- Use the present tense
- Use logical connectives eg: first, in addition, furthermore
- You may use questions or commands eg: Why not …? Think of the benefits of …

Unit of work 9

Mobile Phones for Children

BOY, 10, MUGGED FOR PHONE

'Why can't I have one? All my friends have got them.'

Anna, aged 9

'I gave my daughter a mobile phone for safety reasons, so that she can let me know where she is.'

Parent

'The cost of the phone bills is the biggest problem.'

Parent

Units of work 10

' Recent research has found that young children's health could be at risk through using these phones. '

Doctor

' It really irritates me when mobile phones ring in lessons. '

Teacher

Meat Eating Versus Vegetarianism

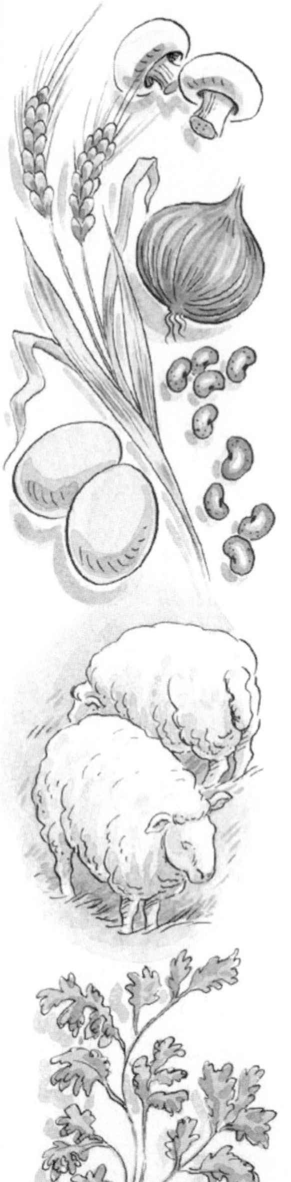

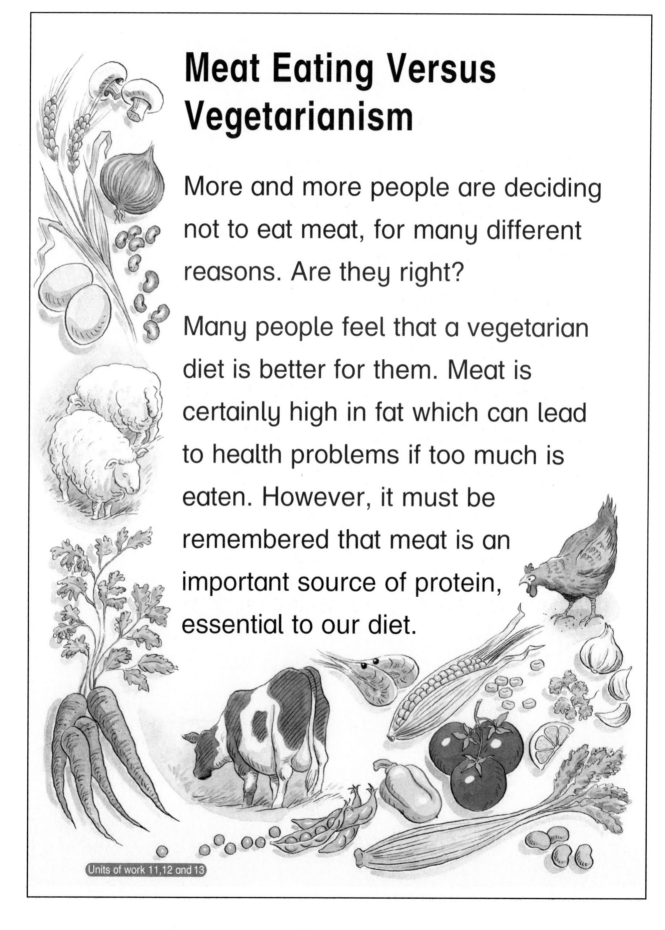

More and more people are deciding not to eat meat, for many different reasons. Are they right?

Many people feel that a vegetarian diet is better for them. Meat is certainly high in fat which can lead to health problems if too much is eaten. However, it must be remembered that meat is an important source of protein, essential to our diet.

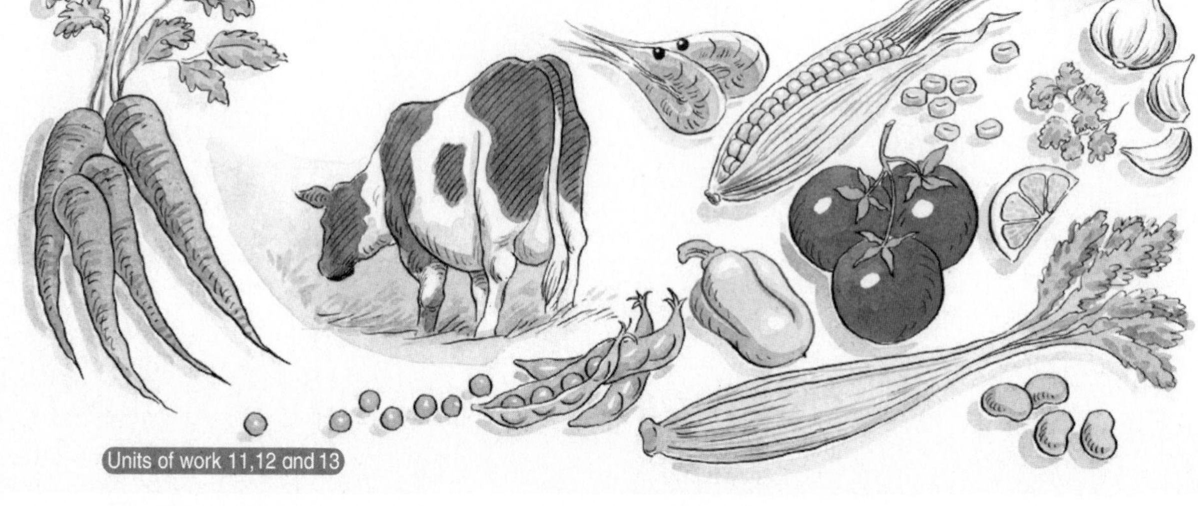

Units of work 11,12 and 13

People are also concerned about the risk of animal diseases such as BSE in cattle, or scrapie in sheep being transferred to humans. Others say this is not proven and are prepared to take the risk.

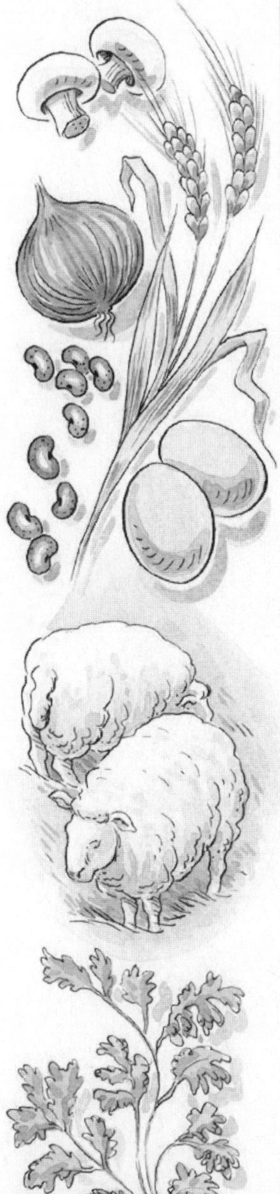

Animal welfare is another important issue. Vegetarians object to animals being kept in confined spaces and force-fed. However, there are strict rules about how animals are fed and looked after, to ensure there is no unnecessary cruelty.

Units of work 11,12 and 13

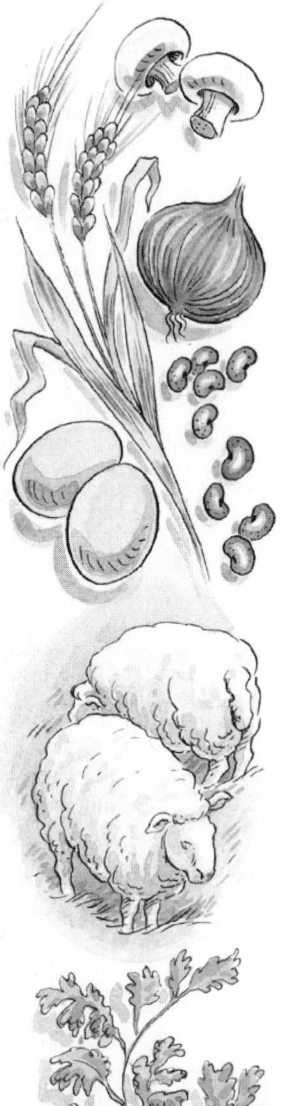

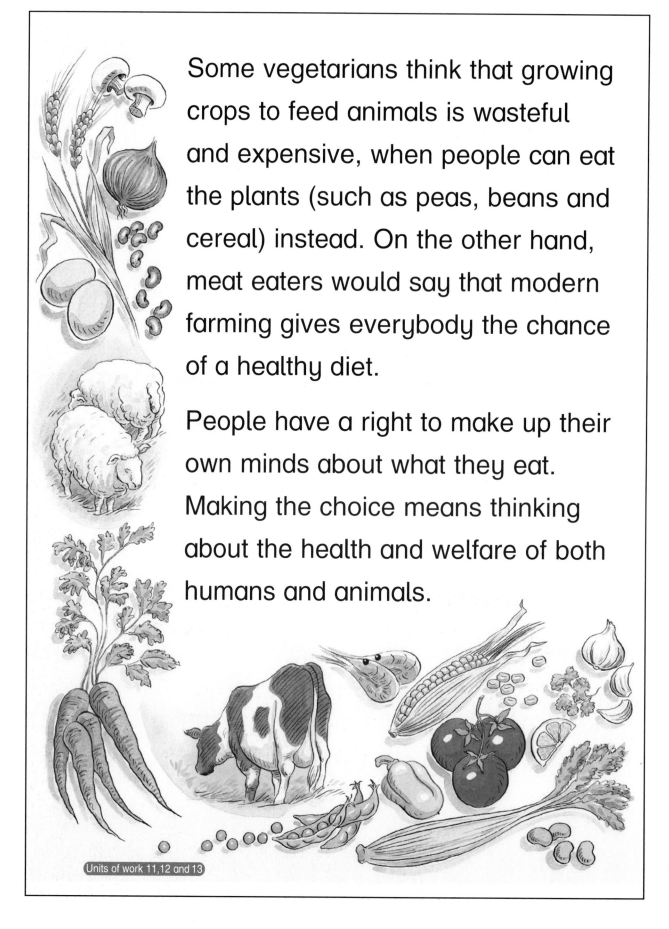

Some vegetarians think that growing crops to feed animals is wasteful and expensive, when people can eat the plants (such as peas, beans and cereal) instead. On the other hand, meat eaters would say that modern farming gives everybody the chance of a healthy diet.

People have a right to make up their own minds about what they eat. Making the choice means thinking about the health and welfare of both humans and animals.

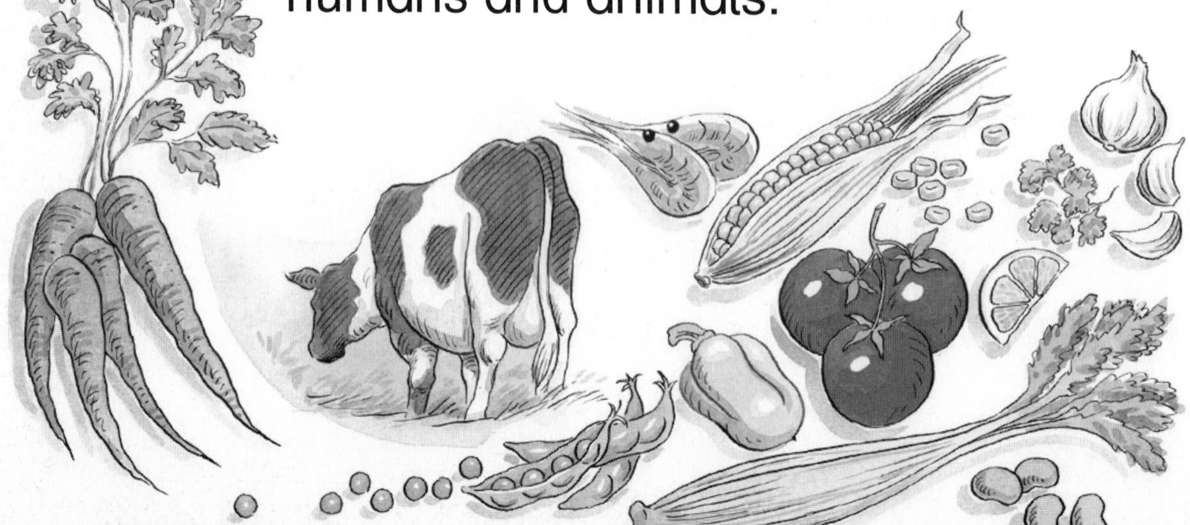

Units of work 11,12 and 13

Writing a Balanced Report

The purpose

- Present both sides of an issue

What to do

- Introduce the issue with a short opening statement
- Put the arguments for and against
- Support each point with evidence
- Don't give one side of the argument more weight than the other
- Summarise the points in a short conclusion

How to write it

- Use the present tense
- Use general subjects eg: 'Some people ...' 'Some children ...'
- Use connectives that contrast, eg: 'However', 'On the other hand'
- Use verbs like 'think' and 'feel'

Units of work 11 and 12

Confusing Notices

Please do not sit babies on the bacon slicer. We are getting behind with our orders.

THIS LAVATORY IS BROKEN. USE THE FLOOR BELOW.

WOMAN HIT BY BUS CRITICAL

SHIP'S CAPTAIN SPOTS MAN EATING FISH

Unit of work 14

Making a Contract

In return for increasing your pocket money, you will have to do more jobs.

Signed: ....

(Parent)

....

(Child)

Date ....

Unit of work 14

TELEVISION WATCHING SURVEY

How many TV sets are there in your house?

How much TV do you watch?

What is your favourite kind of programme?

What is your favourite programme?

Do you have a video recorder?

Who is your favourite person on TV?

What would you like more of?

Writing Paragraphs

Their purpose

- They give structure to the writing and show the reader how the writer's ideas are organised

What to do

- Present a new idea or aspect of the subject in each paragraph
- Start each new paragraph by stating the idea then give examples and/or details
- Make sure each paragraph builds on the one before
- Begin each new paragraph on a new line
- Leave a one-line gap between paragraphs or indent the first line
- Link paragraphs with connectives like 'However', 'Also', 'Therefore'

Unit of work 16

Public Notices

NO SWIMMING IN THE LAKE

KEEP DOGS ON THE LEAD AT ALL TIMES

KEEP OFF THE GRASS

No Smoking

WASH YOUR HANDS BEFORE COOKING

Unit of work 17

CARRY DOGS ON THE ESCALATOR

CLEANING IN PROGRESS

Do not sunbathe on this beach with no clothes on

Do not drive on the motorway with a bag on your head

WEAR A SEAT BELT ON ALL JOURNEYS

How wool yarn is made

Wool yarn is made by pulling fleece into strips. Then the strips are twisted to make them stay together and make them strong.

The twisting process that makes yarn is called spinning. Spinning has been done by hand for over 2,000 years. Some people still spin by hand, but today most wool yarn is spun on machines. Almost any kind of hair can be spun, but the most common is sheep's wool.

Unit of work 18

Two or more different fibres can be mixed together before being spun into a single yarn. This is called a blended yarn.

Writing in different styles and forms

TEXT TYPE	diary	newspaper report	wall display	Formal letter
Recount				
Explanation				
Report				
Instructions				
Persuasion				
Discussion				

informal letter	recipe	instruction leaflet	poster	leaflet

Unit of work 19

Training your dog to 'sit'

For this exercise you will need a training lead.

1. Shorten the training lead so that it is not tight but your dog cannot move forward.

2. With your dog on your left side, hold your lead in your right hand.

3. Press gently but firmly in the dog's hind quarters with your left hand. At the same time, pull gently up on the right, using the command 'sit'.

Units of work 19 and 20

4. When the dog sits, praise it and move out of position.

5. Place the dog on your left again and repeat the exercise. You will soon find that the dog will understand the command 'sit' automatically without your help.

Always remember to praise the dog after it has finished the exercise.

Little Greening Dog Show

Entries for the 24th Little Greening Dog Show on Saturday the 24th were at a record level this year. It was a warm, sunny afternoon for the judges, Mr Harry Dalton and Mrs Joan Murray, and the good-sized crowd of enthusiasts who watched as the pooches were put through their paces by their proud owners.

First in the judging ring were the various breed classes. The winners of these (see below for details) were then judged for 'Best In Show'. Clearly a popular choice, the standard poodle, Trixie, owned by Mrs Jean Harris, was announced as the overall winner and received the Mason trophy for the third year running.

Units of work 19 and 20

The pet classes followed with John Chandler's 'Mack' winning 'Dog with the waggiest tail'; Mr Tom Martin's Labrador 'Bob' was 'the Dog most like its owner' and the dog which the judges would most like to take home was young Emma Clarke's puppy, Jess.

Everyone – dogs, owners, judges and audience – enjoyed the afternoon enormously, a witness to the enduring popularity of the village Dog Show.

Units of work 19 and 20

Dog Illnesses – Heat Stroke

What it is

Dogs can collapse from becoming too hot. This is known as heat stroke.

How it happens

The most common cause is when a dog is shut in a vehicle which is parked in full sun with its windows closed.

The temperature in the car soars so that the dog becomes increasingly hot and therefore distressed and cannot breathe properly.

As the dog's breathing worsens, its temperature rises eventually causing it to collapse.

Units of work 19 and 20

What to do

The dog's temperature should be reduced as quickly as possible by putting it in cold water, hosing it down or rubbing it with ice cubes (or a pack of frozen vegetables).

Do you want your dog to suffocate?

No? then remember to LET THE FRESH AIR IN

If your dog is left in the car, make sure fresh air can circulate by leaving windows slightly open.

Units of work 19 and 20

Year 6 Non-Fiction Cross Curricular Links

	Unit of work	Topics covered	Links
Term 1	1: Write an autobiography (T14)	Samuel Pepys	**Pupils should be taught:** (**History** H1a) to place events, people … into correct periods of time (H5c) to communicate their knowledge and understanding of history in a variety of ways
	2: Write a biography (T14)		
	3: Describe a person (T14)	Roald Dahl	
	4: Write an obituary (T14)		
	5: Develop a journalistic style (T15)	Article about fox	
	6: Write a newspaper report (T16)	Samuel Pepys and the Great Plague	(H5a) recall, select and organise historical information (H5b) use dates and historical vocabulary to describe the periods studied
	7: Write a non-chronological report (T17)	Desert animals	(**Science** Sc2 5b) about the different plants and animals found in different habitats
	8: Revise and edit writing (T18)	Article about fox	
Term 2	9: Compose an argument (T18)	Walking to school	(Sc2 2h) about the importance of exercise for good health.
	10: Present a formal argument (T18)		
	11: Write a balanced report (T19)	Vegetarianism Mobile phones	(Sc2 2b) about the … importance of an adequate and varied diet (**Geography** G1d) to identify and explain different views that people, including themselves, hold
	12: Summarise an argument (S4)		
	13: Make notes (S4)	Walking to school	
	14: Make a contract (T20)	Television Homework	
	15: Write a questionnaire (T20)		
Term 3	16: Divide text into paragraphs (T21)	Olympic Games	(**History** H2c) about the social, cultural … diversity of the societies studied
	17: Write notices (S3)	Public notices	
	18: Write an explanation (T20)	Making wool yarn	(**Design and Technology** DT 5a) to investigate … a range of familiar products
	19: Identify text types (T22)	Dogs	
	20: Select text type (T22)		